Being Human

*Inspiration for Balancing
Mind Body and Spirit*

Tammy Plunkett

BALBOA.
PRESS
A DIVISION OF HAY HOUSE

Balboa Press books may be ordered through booksellers or by contacting:

Balboa Press
A Division of Hay House
1663 Liberty Drive
Bloomington, IN 47403
www.balboapress.com
1-(877) 407-4847

Because of the dynamic nature of the Internet, any web addresses or links contained in this book may have changed since publication and may no longer be valid. The views expressed in this work are solely those of the author and do not necessarily reflect the views of the publisher, and the publisher hereby disclaims any responsibility for them.

The author of this book does not dispense medical advice or prescribe the use of any technique as a form of treatment for physical, emotional, or medical problems without the advice of a physician, either directly or indirectly. The intent of the author is only to offer information of a general nature to help you in your quest for emotional and spiritual well-being. In the event you use any of the information in this book for yourself, which is your constitutional right, the author and the publisher assume no responsibility for your actions.

Any people depicted in stock imagery provided by Thinkstock are models, and such images are being used for illustrative purposes only.
Certain stock imagery © Thinkstock.

Printed in the United States of America

ISBN: 978-1-4525-6958-1 (sc)
ISBN: 978-1-4525-6960-4 (hc)
ISBN: 978-1-4525-6959-8 (e)

Library of Congress Control Number: 2013903661

Balboa Press rev. date: 3/7/2013

To my children, my reason for being

At the center of your being
you have the answer;
you know who you are
and you know what you want.

— *Lao Tzu*

Acknowledgments

I would like to thank all my guides and teachers along my path, too many to name here, but especially Adele Stratton and Dr. Shahram Ayoubsadeh, David and Ahdi Guy, Brian O'Connell, and Dr. Brenda Saxe. If there is any sense of story, grammar, or sentence structure in my work it is thanks to the lessons I learned from my community of writers at the Ottawa Romance Writers' Association and my amazing critique partners and cheerleaders: Brenda Heald, who was instrumental in this project; and past supporters Kris Wong, Lillian Chow, Leeann Lessard; and the lady responsible for starting the process, Joyce Sullivan. I am very grateful to Rachel Hockett for her editorial magic and to Julie Hearty for my gorgeous cover and author photos.

Thank you to my parents and sister for the life lessons that have shaped who I am today. To my husband who listened as I read my book out loud, who never complained about the hours of my nose in a book researching, and most of all who nurtured my dream of being a writer. And to my very precious children who share my love of books and storytelling and love me just the way I am, as I love them unconditionally as well.

Preface

The Story about Stories

> *Placing the blame or judgment on someone else leaves you powerless to change your experience; taking responsibility for your beliefs and judgments gives you the power to change them.*
>
> — *Byron Katie*

Once upon a time...

Marlene shielded her sister's body with her own as their father, Paul, swung a hunting rifle through the air and threatened to shoot their border collie over something he believed Marlene had done.

"It's going to be okay, Diane. God is not going to let us die like this. Not like this. He's watching over us. We're going to be okay." She whispered in her sister's ear.

The dog barked frantically at their dad's aggressiveness, and their mother edged around the room trying to quiet it.

Finally, their mom spoke. "Put the gun down, Paul. For Christ's sake, she says she didn't make out with a boy."

Although Marlene had no idea who or what God was, somehow she knew she had spoken the truth to her sister. She knew they wouldn't die. There was no logical explanation for her revelation, and definitely no divine intervention in the past that would have given her the comfort of God's presence. She didn't hear His voice in her head. She didn't see an angel bathed in a warm golden glow. She just knew, at that very moment, for the first time in her life, that something was protecting her, that something loved her, and that something had bigger plans for her than to be murdered by a deluded abuser. The revelation gave Marlene peace, and transformed her from the lead actor in a slow and plotless horror film into a distanced spectator who had the power to change the channel.

The eight and fifteen-year-old sisters remained huddled on the couch. The familiar scent of cigarette smoke mingled with alcohol fumes laced the dry overheated air. Marlene held the sobbing Diane in her arms, stared at the wood paneling's fake knots, and listened to her mother try to reason with a madman. In the dim light of the living room, the knots looked like tears and she knew those walls had a lot to cry about.

"You think I'm stupid?" Paul's European accent grew thicker with rage. "She kissed him and he wiped his mouth on her shirt! I know what I see. It's the same color as her lipstick."

"Her best friend, Julie, has the same lipstick. They bought it together. She must have hugged Marlene and got some on her shirt."

"I'm not stupid!" He smashed the butt of the rifle through the glass door of the china cabinet. The sound of cascading glass was a backdrop to their mother's gasp. Her whole body trembled like a kite in a windstorm. The deadly silence that followed seemed to crystallize the drama into reality.

Somehow, Marlene dared to speak.

"That is what happened, Dad, I didn't kiss a boy. I promise." It was the truth. She had danced one slow dance with Louis—the object of her teen hormonal affection—at the ninth-grade Valentine's Day dance. They had not kissed. Yet guilt ravaged a hole in her stomach. She knew full well that forbidden male attention had triggered this terrible fight.

In her father's mind, Marlene belonged to him. The thought of her dancing and kissing another man—in this case a mere boy—drove him insane. While she knew with every single cell of her being that his definition of fatherhood was wrong and felt absolutely disgusting, she also knew better than to ask other people's opinions about whether his actions were appropriate.

The gun never fired that night, the dog lived to see another day and they all went on with the charade. Their father left the room after Marlene said she hadn't kissed anyone and went for a long cooling-off drive. Diane and Marlene went to bed, and their mom cleaned the whole scene spotless and then took a Valium. She spent that Sunday in bed with the curtains drawn, feigning another migraine. They didn't go to church. They never went to church. Yet the feeling of deeper meaning that Marlene only knew to call God stayed with her.

I share this story because I grew up in a similar environment. I have personally learned since then that I am not my story, and Marlene is not her story, and that Paul was choosing the role of a bad guy. With this book I hope to accentuate the point that we have to choose to insert more being into our human lives—otherwise we live as little more than animals. Paul was a predatory animal, and Marlene was his prey until she came into her spiritual being-ness and managed to thrive fully. From my own life lessons and by seeing things for what they really are, by gaining a sense of having a higher self that is connected to a power greater than me, and by choosing, repeatedly and consciously, to reconcile my basic human drives, my higher consciousness, and my spiritual existence, I have learned to live a free and peaceful life despite many more challenges that have sprung up along the way.

This is only a tiny glimpse into the type of life I endured as a child and young adult. Yet I not only survived that part of my story, I flourished. I moved out at the age of nineteen, worked three jobs to put myself through nursing school, became a professional, got married, bought a house and a car, and had two children—all by the time I was twenty-seven years old—while the rest of my family struggled with conflict, barely surviving. I don't know why I found a connection to spiritual being-ness during tumultuous times while my family did not. I do know, however, that it changed my life to one of more peace and less struggle.

Like Marlene, I have never heard the voice of God nor have I seen an angel bathed in a warm glow on the nights of horrors I have survived, but I truly believe that a higher power has guided me through Oprah Winfrey on many occasions. She introduced me to Deepak Chopra and his book *Quantum Healing*, which molded my nursing and then alternative healing careers. She introduced me to Marianne Williamson's *A Return to Love*, which was the first of my many life-changing, inspirational reads. And Oprah introduced me to the fact that I wasn't alone; she introduced me to the many other people in the world who have suffered equal or greater atrocities than I—she told me their stories.

If we go back to the opening story and delve into Paul's character development, it makes the story more believable if he was abused as a child as well. It is a well-known phenomenon that abusers often were abused or had it modeled for them growing up. Imagine that his father did horrific things to him and said horrific things about him and Paul chose to live out that story and embrace the thought that he was a bad guy, and that the only love he could ever have was from someone he could control. But essentially, Paul, Marlene and I are equals before our stories separate us. We all start off as humans who must choose to lift our consciousness every moment of every day, or not.

My own resilience comes from the realization that these are stories.

That does not mean our stories didn't really happen. That does not mean the resulting physical, emotional, and psychological pain is not real. But our stories are not who we are. You and I have a choice all the time to live the role in the story or to be who we are deep down inside—spiritual potential.

I know I had a crappy childhood; my memory tells me so. My body knows it was hurt, but it has regenerated itself many times since then, hasn't it? Do I live in the same body now that was mistreated twenty-five years ago? Science tells us that my cells have renewed. I can tell you my belly isn't as flat and has a lot of stretch marks that weren't there, and I'm pretty sure I wouldn't be able to fit into a single piece of clothing that I wore back when I was ten or sixteen either (there seems to be a lot more of me now).

So if my body isn't really the same, and I am going off a memory of something that hasn't happened in twenty-five years, how can that be who I am now? How can it be anything but a story held in my memory and brought back to life every time I recount the story either out loud or to myself in my inner dialogue? And if it is a story, can I not simply allow myself to turn the page and write a new one for the present moment?

During the worst of all that I endured in my life, I never identified myself as a victim, and I don't see myself now as ever having been victimized. It was part of my journey through life and my lessons to learn. I believe that what some people would call horrors from my past are only mileposts on my road to where I am today.

And my message is that none of us can overcome tragedy or even navigate everyday life in a healthy and effective way if we don't merge our human with our being. Embracing my being has been my saving grace, and I'd love to share with you how you can find your peace and happiness through embracing your human being-ness.

My life has changed quite a bit from when I was twenty-seven years old. I went through a divorce twelve years ago and a few years after that I left the nursing profession, remarried, and became a stay-at-home mother. During this time I studied everything, from homeopathy, to psychology, to creative writing, to intuitive healing. While I have consistently been drawn to the spirituality I found at age fourteen and built on it through the years, I have also lived in today's world of achievement, materialism, and status, and that world is not one that is easily ignored or forgotten. I can truly say that when I turned forty, I went from wanting to "be good" for the sole reason of seeking approval, to wanting to be balanced for the sake of humanity.

My calling has always been to teach and inspire, and to reframe what others didn't understand. I can remember being a keen student and when a fellow student didn't understand something the teacher said, I would cut in and explain it using different words. I'm sure it drove my teachers nuts, but I always had a passion to enlighten others and help them understand.

So now, I make it my goal in life to help others find their own answers, to hear the words of the wise men and women who have come before me, and to incorporate the many teachings of our day and age to enhance their lives.

I want others to see their stories as part of their past no matter how distant or recent. I want others to see that they have new choices and new options open to them all the time. And I want people to be okay with being human. We need to accept both parts of who we are, and both parts of who everyone is. There is a good reason that so many faiths and cultures speak of two parts of the whole, from yin and yang, to mother Earth and father sky, to the ego and the soul. We need both parts. Let's live the experience and learn to be human.

Introduction

The Human Being

Man is the only creature who refuses to be what he is.

—Albert Camus

THE TITLE FOR *BEING HUMAN* CAME to be while I was meditating after a yoga session in the late summer of 2011. At the time my life was a walk in the park. We were financially comfortable and everyone in my family was healthy. In fact, I had recently lost a bunch of excess weight by eliminating sugar from my diet and joining the gym where I was now meditating. My children were doing well in school, I was relaunching my health and wellness consulting business after a six-year hiatus, my oldest daughter had a boyfriend I finally approved of. Life was grand.

Part of my plans around launching my business included writing a book. I always have a book in the back of my mind waiting to be typed out and offered to the world, and I thought it was the perfect time for me to help the world become healthy, happy, and motivated. But there was this enormous seed of insecurity that surreptitiously danced around in my brain: "You are not an expert. You don't have the credentials. There are no letters in front of or behind your name. You have no authority to write a book." Then it came to me as I breathed deeply on my yoga mat under the dim lighting of the gym, "I know all about being human. No one can say otherwise. I've always been one and I know exactly what it's like. I will write about being human."

So I went home and started jotting down all the things I thought I was doing right to have such a bowl of cherries for a life. I have known hardship in my lifetime and I wanted to give the gift of peace to those who were going through anything like what I had experienced in my younger years.

And then life happened.

First, an injured foot kept me from maintaining my prior fitness program; then my daughter broke up with the "good" boyfriend and started hanging-out with the "bad" crowd. I used food to cope with what was potentially the most stressful period of my life, and quickly put on forty pounds. And it all culminated in an evening when I crossed my own prominent line in the sand, and made a choice. Many people wouldn't bat an eye at this choice or would call it a mistake; some people would tsk and wag a finger at it; most people would probably chalk it up to a moment of weakness, and say: "You were just being human, nobody is perfect." But the next day, I was devastated.

I was invited over to a friend's house for a celebratory glass of champagne. I don't drink alcohol. And as you read this book and the impact others' drinking has had on my life, and the absolute epidemic of addiction in my family, you will understand why. But there are other reasons too. I hold a belief that alcohol interferes with our ability to be spiritual and close to Source, and least of all, alcohol—the kind I would like to drink if I were to drink—is packed with sugar. I put on forty pounds by indulging in the things I taught people in health classes to avoid at all cost. Go figure.

I am not a temperance movement banner waver. It is my personal choice. I had the rare social glass of wine or martini in my adult life prior to that night, always living with the fear and knowing on a deep level that every glass I drank was putting me at the top of a steep and icy slippery slope.

My husband and I went to a six-week support group meeting for parents of troubled teens, where we were asked to take a vow of sobriety for those six weeks to show solidarity for our teens and to lead by example. I thought it would be a breeze. The evening that I went over to my friend's house was five weeks into the program, things were extremely stressful with my fifteen-year-old daughter who struggled with a chronic illness and had left home several times, and I was at my wits' end. So there I sat with two exceptionally intelligent and funny ladies sipping wine and discussing all kinds of things from equal distribution of household chores among two working parents to sex toys in Happy Meals. I laughed so hard my cheeks and sides hurt for days. I didn't have a care in the world and I hadn't felt that way for at least a year. I also drank more alcohol in one evening than I had since in all the days since college. I had to call my husband to come pick me up to drive me home one block because I could not have walked that far without falling over. This was so out of character for me that he was worried enough to ask me to speak to our daughter's counselor about it. I spent the night hugging white porcelain and the next day I couldn't look at myself in the mirror.

I was just a human being, but I made the decision that day to start concentrating on my being-ness and to find a way to live as a human who can look in the mirror daily. This book represents what I have found, so far.

Human beings are very complex, as any biologist or psychologist will tell you. I love to watch videos that show the progression of a human life from conception through forty weeks. How a cell suddenly splits in half is amazing, then it continues to multiply itself over and over, each cell developing into the proper organ in the proper place. Having been a cardiac nurse, I am particularly fond of how fast the heart develops into the four chambers that work in perfect unison to clean the blood of carbon dioxide and feed the body with oxygen. By the time a baby is born, 60,000 miles of blood vessels have developed to assist in that delivery and removal system. It's not only awe inspiring, it is also tremendously complicated. Most of our biological systems are automatic—we don't have to think about making our heart beat; we have deep innate drives to maintain homeostasis—or balance—to breathe, drink water, and eat.

We also have spectacularly evolved thoughts that we are able to communicate to others in various ways. Our mind is as much of a marvel as our body in its capacity to learn, unlearn, believe, and perceive. Take phantom limb pain, for example; I have witnessed firsthand where a perfectly sane man felt his foot after a below-the-knee amputation. He knew there was no longer a foot there, but his

4

mind still felt it. Another medical condition, seemingly opposite to phantom limb, was recently made well known through Lisa Genova's novel, *Left Neglect*. This happens when someone's brain fails to recognise body parts that are there and fully functional. But what has been the most mind-blowing for me recently (pardon the pun) was learning that patients with multiple personality disorders can actually manifest diseases in only one personality and not have that disease at all in the other personalities—and not only symptoms, but medically diagnosed diseases. This phenomenon is being studied as an indication of how much our beliefs affect our physical body. There is compelling evidence from bone fide science labs showing us what award-winning physicist John Wheeler speculated: Reality is created by observers in the Universe.

Many of us live in a world that navigates mostly on autopilot, leaving everything up to our body's automatic systems and our animalistic drives: Eat, have sex to propagate our genes, and survive. We may think we are more evolved than animals, but for some of us the day-in, day-out routine of going to work to make money to buy stuff, come home, eat, watch television, and have sex on Wednesdays and Saturdays is not all that much more enlightened than the rabbit snacking on the vegetables in the garden. We have to wonder sometimes if we are the more enlightened ones with some of the choices we make as humans, when some of our choices affect so many on a grander scale. Two bucks smashing horns together over a female or a piece of territory hurt fewer people and animals than the wars we humans wage over our beliefs.

I want to underline that humans are very different from animals even though I refer to our animalistic side. Humans are called sentient yet animals also have senses that are even more acute then ours—a dog's sense of smell is 100,000 times stronger than a human's, and an eagle's sense of sight is keener than that of a human's. Our human senses are much more important in terms of perception and interpretation. We as humans make discoveries in all sciences: We discovered and used fire and discovered metals, we invented tools, created cameras to take pictures and musical instruments to produce art. Only humans perceive themselves and things that are not outward, such as intellectual concepts, love and sorrow, and spirituality. This perception and identification of things we cannot sense is what separates humans from other animals. This is what many people define as spirituality. This is not a matter of abasing animals. We all have pets and other animals in our lives for whom we care immensely, and I am not saying they are not valuable parts of our lives. Just as with everything in spirituality we all have a varying degree of belief and I know that many people believe that their pets have a soul and will meet them on the other side. That might very well be a truth. However, we must acknowledge the higher order of the human being and the impact the human mind and creativity has had on our world—for better and for worse.

To the animalistic side of us, the other side of humans—the more evolved side—should look great in theory. I've never seen two cats dance the tango or a horse tell his grandson about the day he graduated at the top of his class. Our sentient and conscious minds are amazing. However, many will argue that while some monks are able to sit on a mountainside and meditate their whole lives, it is not a practical occupation for the whole of humanity. We may have more evolved minds than the rabbits, but we still are physical beings, and somebody has to stop meditating long enough to cook dinner. Therein lays the quest of us humans since the birth of spiritual pursuits: How to be in the world but not of it?

This book will show us the fine balance, the fluid dance between our drives and our higher selves. Human beings cannot forsake their human shell and their bodily functions to be completely enlightened beings. We need both, the vessel and the higher self, the human and the being. The goal is to find balance between both—to blend both.

Can I still be in the moment and completely conscious if I overindulge in a pan of warm, gooey brownies? Yes. Can I sustain my highest level of enlightenment if I indulge in said pan on a daily basis? Well, it depends. Am I ensuring a healthy diet the rest of the day, and adequate exercise to maintain a well body? Is my body, or, more importantly, my mind to the point where it needs that pan of brownies? How much of my day is spent longing for the brownies? Has it become a mindless habit or a subconscious drive? Do you see the slippery slope? And we are just talking about dessert.

What happens when the world we live in is solely focused on the physical aspect? Only on what it can see and feel? Some people think what goes on inside the four walls of their house with their family only affects the people physically in that room. But it doesn't. It affects the whole Universe. More and more emerging studies show that we are all connected by quantum energy fields, and that what one person does actually affects the whole.

And then we get mixed messages about melding spirituality with physical needs. Food and sex are by far the human being's strongest drives. They represent the survival instinct and the survival of our genetic make-up. Most religious creeds promote conservative views on sex: only after marriage, not too much of it, and by all means don't have any fun doing it. Yet, many religions also ask us to go forth and reproduce, and discourage the use of contraceptives. So what's the deal? Do the enlightened ones think we should be embracing or suppressing one of our strongest physical drives?

That's a bit of a trick question. We will be looking into how our society views and creates beliefs around all of our drives. I don't feel that it is an absolute given that religious leaders are necessarily enlightened, there are some—not all—who are more attracted to power and wealth and human gains of the Earth than a connection to Source. The prophets were enlightened, of course, and they too addressed the duality of man.

There are two parts to the human being, the matter and the spirit. We have spent a lot of time concentrating on the matter in our recent history—a lot of time studying the laws of physics, geography, and biology. We invented microscopes and machines to study and build things to make our physical lives better. We have studied and measured everything that we could manipulate. However, we also invented things that we can't see: the digital waves that connect our cell phones and Wi-Fi that allows us to learn about things we never could have imagined learning about. We punch a term into a search engine (note the word "engine," from our machine days) and within seconds we are given a whole new world of information. It has taken a while for some of the matter-focused scientists to embrace the World Wide Web, and there is a plethora of untested and unproven information. It is very difficult for people who are entrenched in their beliefs to accept proof of things just because someone else said it was so; this reluctance is justified, because there is also a large body of beliefs that need testing.

Despite those focused on the physical, we have begun studying spirituality en masse at the beginning of the twenty-first century. We have disrobed the dogma of religion and searched for a core truth that can be translated to any religion and faith. And this new spiritual study coincides with scientific discoveries. "Quantum nonlocality" in essence shows an entanglement and interconnectedness of the Universe on a microscopic level, and you can look into almost every religion and all spiritual practices and find references to the notion that "we are all one."

So as a society of scientists and spiritual seekers, we are ready to make a union between the human and the being.

If we are all born human beings, then we must all have the potential to thrive in our duality. Why do some of us bounce back from setbacks, learn lessons the first or second time we are faced with an issue, or some even seem to sail through life unscathed? That is one of the questions I am posing with this book. The only time I have ever known anyone to flourish is when they embraced both the human part and the being part.

The main thing that separates humans from other animals is our sense and ability for perception. I am not going to argue if animals feel grief or happiness. They are as capable of the biochemistry as humans are, but I cannot see that they are as conscious of these emotions and able to judge them in context as we do. We don't know which organ, if any, perception resides in, but the mind/brain interprets and converts perception into brain chemistry, which is released into the bloodstream and affects cellular behavior—this area of scholarship is called epigenetics and is being perfected by Dr. Bruce Lipton and Deepak Chopra.

Perceptions of love release dopamine, oxytocin, and vasopressin, which create a medium that enhances cell function and growth. Perceptions of fear release a cascade of stress hormones—norepinephrine, histamine, cytokines, and cortisol, which in turn shut down the immune system and cellular growth.

Humans have many physical needs and distractions that drive us on a daily basis. We all need to eat, for example, and if you go hungry or are on food restriction of any kind, your body soon shows you precisely how physically and psychologically dependent you are on food. When you get hungry enough little else occupies your mind besides getting the next meal; with thirst, it's the next drink of water.

And as far as sex is concerned, we get to thank the plethora of hormones that kick in when we become teenagers. Our bodies, like every other species, have a strong drive to reproduce and propel the species.

Besides food and sex, what are some of the other needs and distractions that drive us? And notice my use of the words "distractions" and "drive." The physical body in its basic state needs to eat, but there is no innate *drive* to play solitaire on the computer; that is an innocuous distraction from life that many of us use on a regular basis. For a few, playing cards becomes a compulsion, and a need that drives their lives. Addiction wears many hats, from the socially unacceptable heroin addict on the streets of an inner city to the socially applauded workaholic who makes his first million before he is thirty.

We will look at these human traits and more, including competition, clinging to identities, ego, and cultural promotion of the desire to see others fail. Are we all doomed to these humanistic qualities, or can we rise above them by being more dualistic?

Now about the being side of us. Let me explain the words I will be using interchangeably in this book. To quote the great Alan Watts, "You can't get wet by the word water." And I do hope that whatever words I use don't offend the reader. I will interchangeably use "physical," "vessel," "animalistic," and "human" to describe our more primal selves. I will also use the words "enlightened," "mindful," and "spiritual" for our higher selves. If I mention the words "God," "Universe," "Creator," or "Source," please see them as attempts to describe my view and perspective—the quality of the water without getting you wet. All beings have beliefs, even atheists believe in the scientific method or ethics in society, and this book is as much for an atheist and it is for a religious person. All are welcome here.

The being part of the human is the part that rises above its innate drives and finds a deeper meaning to its existence. And really, is that not one of our more frequently asked questions? Why am I here? I am here to be.

Being is going with the flow and not resisting the process of life, being is doing with intent and meaning, being is existing in the present moment and dealing with the truth of the here and now, being is peace, love and acceptance, and community and harmony.

And because being is made of all these wonderful qualities, many religions and spiritual leaders have given it a higher value than our human side. They have made it the good against which we measure the bad, and anyone who is not living solely in the realm of what I call being is considered by many spiritual leaders to be weak, a sinner, even evil.

I'm not buying it. I'm not buying that we are meant to pit ourselves against ourselves, that we are expected to negate everything that comes along with being human to be angelic. Why would we be given human bodies and put on Earth if we were supposed to act like perfect spiritual beings? I have heard and actually can buy into the idea of trying to create heaven on Earth by being more like God (or his Prophets, or his Son, depending on your religion) and I do believe that by embracing our being-ness we are working toward that goal, and that embracing our being-ness is what our journey on Earth is all about. But there are limits, and there are extremes. And what I have learned from my life is that extremes don't allow for a good balance. If we are to balance both our sides we will have to stay away from extremes.

While I shall touch on both sides of being human, I will point out the tendency for us to give into the human part much more easily. I don't want it to seem that I am pushing for one side more than the other. However, we live in a world much more geared to the instant gratification of our physical side, and our physical DNA has been on this planet much longer than our enlightenment. Living organisms have been around for 545 million years, and humans are thought to have only showed up in the last twenty thousand years. That's a lot more nonsentient DNA history.

Our biology is the building block and genetic blueprint for the vessel that holds our mind and consciousness. Our DNA and genes do not have self-actualization. Our body requires a contractor to use those blueprints to build our life. We are the contractors. We have the control if we can be conscious of our thoughts. And this is the answer of how to *be* human.

So we are dealing with both the past and the present skewing our guiding forces for balance, and as such I may have to sound a little biased at times. But I will try to interject some pleas for equality and avoidance of extremes every once in a while.

Last, this book was not written from start to finish in sequence, and it doesn't have to be read that way. If you are dying to find out what I have written about being human in a sexual context feel free to jump ahead. I do suggest you read the whole book at some point, however, as the lessons included here will greatly assist us all in reconciling our basic drives and our higher selves.

PART 1

Biology

Chapter 1

Mind

Freedom means you are unobstructed in living your
life as you choose. Anything less is a form of slavery.
—*Wayne Dyer*

ONE OF THE JOYS OF BEING human is our wonderful ability to be conscious of the world around us. Our conscious mind is perception. It is the part that is aware in the present moment. To be conscious means to be tuned in to what's going on in the now. Our human consciousness is also aware of itself, it is what makes us unique and identify with ourselves—I, Tarzan, you, Jane—it is being conscious of who we are in this vast Universe of stuff. The conscious mind is also what makes us creative, allowing us to invent tools to help with our daily lives and create beautiful stories to entertain the masses. It is not necessarily time bound to the present moment as it allows us to recall a memory from the past or have aspirations for the future.

Let me paraphrase the great Bruce Lipton, PhD, a stem cell biologist and great leader in the field of epigenetics. In scans, the conscious mind is seen working in the prefrontal cortex of the brain—the part in charge of executive function, higher thought, planning, and moderating our behaviors; it accounts for 5 percent of your metal activity and processes information at a speed of about forty nerve impulses per second.

Our subconscious mind, in contrast, accounts for 95 percent of our mental activity and fires at 40,000,000 nerve impulses per second. Our subconscious is thought to be located in our reptilian brain—the part of our brain that has the deepest instinctive drives, also known as our basal ganglia, in charge of procedural learning relating to routine behaviors or habits. It has no identity, it has no self, as it is merely a place that holds information from experiences that it records and plays back, so, for example, we don't have to relearn how to ride a bike every time we get on one, and we know that a poisonous berry is poisonous every time we see it.

The subconscious is where we find our innate drives, where we learn to fear. Fear is an important emotion for the survival of man and it is a driving force for everything the subconscious does. The subconscious mind starts to acquire programming from the third trimester in utero by bathing in the neurochemicals released during the love and fear responses from the mother. Then even more so in the first six years of life when the child's brain is in a more receptive state to subconscious learning than at any other time in life. And this is when enculturation occurs. Let me tell you two stories, one about leaning to fear and the other about enculturation.

I grew up in a working-class family. We moved around a lot. I never attended any school for more than two years, with the exception of our four-year stay in Hemmingford, Quebec. When we moved in, we lived in a trailer. It was a permanent trailer that was fixed to a basement, but a trailer nonetheless. It evolved, however, as my stepfather renovated and moved room walls and expanded it, so that by the time we moved out, our trailer looked like an actual house.

The basement was initially on a dirt floor, before all the renovations and transformations. One hot summer day, as we were doing some yard work, my stepfather asked me to go fetch a shovel in the basement. I walked down the couple of steps from the outside door and waited for my eyesight to adjust from the bright sun. It was considerably cooler than outdoors, a little damp, and the air was ripe with the scent of moldy earth. A bare bulb hung from the ceiling lighting my way to the tools hanging on the pegboard wall. And despite the cool and the break in the laborious work, I couldn't wait to get back out in the sunlight. This place was creepy. On my way back out, as I crossed the threshold to the grassy side yard a garter snake slithered over my sandaled foot. I am sure the chills that ran down my back could have been visible had anyone been there to watch. Without a second thought, I screeched, sliced down with the shovel and decapitated that poor little snake in one foul blow. My fight-or-flight response was swift and precise. I fought, and the bigger animal with the sharp tool won.

Oddly enough, I do not have a phobia of snakes. I don't own one as a pet, mind you, but they don't bother me to the point where I can't pet one at a reptile zoo or look at them on television. I do, however, have a strong dislike for basements. Despite having a beautifully finished rec room in the basement of my own home, I only go down there if I absolutely have to. I don't break out in a sweat or have heart palpitations; I just don't like it, and I avoid my basement and basements everywhere as much as I possibly can.

I tell you this story as an example of how our subconscious memories of past events influence our actions today. I can guarantee there are no snakes in my basement today, no creepy crawlies, and no dirt floor, and yet my subconscious helps me avoid going there because of a memory. My conscious mind takes in the present moment, the present surroundings, and can see there are no threats. I can consciously choose to go to the basement without any repercussions. But if I am not consciously choosing to go downstairs I tend not to go.

This tiny little piece of my idiosyncrasies opens a window into how the subconscious mind has a hold on our life if we are not operating from our conscious mind as much as possible. But there is another more surreptitious way our subconscious has a hold on our life, and for me becoming conscious of it takes a lot more work than walking down a flight of stairs to the basement of my house.

Back to my working-class family. By age sixteen, we'd moved from the trailer-now-house out in the country back to the city. We lived in an apartment complex where my grandparents and several of my aunts and uncles and cousins also lived. My stepfather was in jail and my mother worked as a waitress until two o'clock in the morning to pay for the roof over our heads and the food on our table. I was a straight-A student and worked weekend evenings cleaning offices; I was snarkily nicknamed "Goody-Two-Shoes" by all my cousins. I grew up being called a snob with, with the unspoken taunt, "you think you're better than we are." That was the seed planted into my subconscious. That seed is in many of us who have heard the words, "Who do you think you are?" But one day, in particular, I myself dumped a load of fertilizer on that seed, and today I continue to battle what so many have called the *tapes in our head* as a result of it, as evidenced by my self-talk on the yoga mat in the introduction of this book.

My mother and I stood face to face in the small living room of our apartment. The room was bright with midday light coming in from the patio door. We were engaged in a heated argument, the origin of which eludes me, but the anger and indignation coursed through my veins as I yelled and flailed my arms to punctuate my statements. Then I said the life-altering phrase. I spat out: "I am going to grow up to be more than just *a waitress.*"

The wounded look on my mother's face is forever ingrained in my subconscious as the loudest reminder, which often screams to me: "You may think you are better than the rest of us, but you're not!"

I went on to be the first of all my family to pursue higher education, I became a professional, I owned my own car and house. But I couldn't shake the feeling that I didn't deserve any of it, that I was an imposter, that I was raised working class and should always remember I would never be anything but a working-class girl.

The terms "self-sabotage" and "fear of success" get used a lot in motivational circles, and with good reason—many of us are holding ourselves back. I would hear it, I would intellectualize it, I would choose not to hold myself back from all that I wanted, but my subconscious mind never failed to repeat the old tapes whenever I wasn't paying attention. And it wasn't until I sat down with myself and had a real good look at who I was in that present moment that I could see that my subconscious was—is—wrong.

This was part of my enculturation. I was told more often than not that I was different from the normal I grew up in, that by wanting a professional career I was weird and a snob. The normal that had been ingrained in me when my brain was the most receptive to the cues in my environment was to work a menial job just to get by, to party on weekends to forget the woes of life, and to go back to work on Monday and start the grind all over again. In my family, there was no mention of service to others, no religion or spirituality, no planning for the future for myself or the rest of humanity; in fact, the rest of humanity didn't even register on anyone's radar that I was aware of as a child. It's a good idea to stop and think for a while about what you were raised to believe. How true do those beliefs ring to your highest self? What is our highest self, you ask?

For now, and in brief:
1. Our highest self is found in our consciousness.
2. Our highest self is found when we are in the present moment.
3. Our highest self operates out of deliberate intention and not reactiveness.

Enculturation runs deep. That is where racism is bred, that is where hatred and fear lie dormant, and when you are not judging a situation from the conscious mind you risk having someone else's untested beliefs dictate your reaction. I can't say that enough. When you are thinking a thought, where does it come from? Is it your deepest truth or something your subconscious picked up along the way?

Before I answer those questions let's have a closer look at our deep-seated physical drives.

Chapter 2

Food

Treat yourself as if you already are enough. Walk as if you are enough. Eat as if you are enough. See, look, listen as if you are enough. Because it's true.

—*Geneen Roth*

EATING IS A STRONG DRIVE FOR survival, and falls under the definition of a living organism: the capacity to grow, metabolize (for which humans require food, water, and air), respond to stimuli, adapt, and reproduce. My life path has included working as a registered nurse in critical and cardiac care, and then a journey through studying and practicing some alternative healing methods. One of the hats I have worn has been that of health and wellness consultant. Let me introduce you to a composite of my typical client.

Nancy came to see me with the goal of losing half her body weight. She worked in sales, was on the road all day, and ate out of her car most of the time or skipped meals and binged when she got home. She had recently been diagnosed with sleep apnea. Her doctor prescribed a CPAP machine—a breathing mask that pushes air into your lungs while you sleep so that if you stop breathing while you sleep, you are forced to take the next breath.

She was not given a choice, even though she asked her doctor if there was anything else she could do besides sleep with a mask on. He told her that he could not in good conscience allow her to have a driver's license on the scant amount of poor-quality sleep she got nightly. She would be a danger to the public. In addition to the uncomfortable and noisy machine this single woman got to take to bed with her at night, the doctor urged that if she were to lose weight, she could lose the mask and eliminate the threat of losing her driver's license and, by extension, her job.

That was what brought Nancy to my office. She was being asked to lose 160 pounds—a whole other person—and all she could tell me was that she had tried every diet known to humanity, and nothing worked for her. Before she even started she told me she couldn't lose the weight, that as a single woman whose livelihood depended on her keeping her driver's license, and whose romantic life depended on not having to sleep with a machine every night (her words, not mine), she was doomed to never losing the identity of obesity. That was what I was supposed to fix with a diet plan. Ha!

As a health and wellness consultant, I can tell you that most women and an increasing number of men that booked appointments with me were more interested in losing weight than in anything else.

Oh yes, they would come in saying they have chronic back or knee problems, or wanted to regulate their cholesterol or blood sugar, and my favorite catchphrase, they didn't want a diet, they wanted a "lifestyle change," to eat healthier. But what they really wanted was to fit the societal norm of anything but fat. Well, that should be easy, right? I should tell them what to eat, and how much to eat, and voilà, they would drop the pounds, level off their cholesterol and blood sugar, and enjoy all the perks of a healthier lifestyle. It's all about calories in calories out, right? Not exactly.

Even I, who can teach others what to eat and how much to eat, am not waltzing around town in what society regards as the perfect body type. Let me say that again: what society regards as the perfect body type. Even so, there are people who have issues with medically defined obesity, and despite what our society dictates as the norm, they are not well, and need to address their relationships with food.

But first, let me say this is not a weight-loss plan or diet book. I am sharing my view of the human condition. If resistance to weight loss is an issue for you, I strongly advise you to seek professional help for the possible underlying causes.

Let's go through the layers of complex issues Nancy was dealing with. First, Nancy was addicted to food. Not only did she have the normal drive to eat in order to survive, she also took great pleasure and comfort from eating. She then felt shame and guilt for the quantity of food she ate and for the size of her body, but she had no other way of feeling pleasure and comfort except to eat again, and so she cycled over and over. Most of the time Nancy was unconscious of her overeating. She started eating a meal out of hunger and then kept eating for something to do, or to fill an emotional void.

There is a recent and very important discovery of brain centers affected by addiction and the neurotransmitters involved in the addiction process. There also seems to be a genetic component to addiction, a subject to which I devote a whole chapter in this book. For now, let's looks at dopamine and its function in our body. Dopamine is a brain chemical that is responsible for reward-driven learning (what I focus on here) as well as important roles in behavior, sleep, voluntary movement, attention, mood, and working memory. Reward-driven learning refers to a behavior that makes us feel good, so we do more of it. For example, when we train a puppy to sit for a treat, or when we take an illicit drug and get "high," we want to have that experience again. Dopamine also seems to have a role in making some stimuli (like eating a brownie) more prominent options than others. The neuroscience term for this is *saliency*, a key issue in the development of addiction.

I am going into this detail so we can refute the common claim that Nancy simply needs to put down the doughnut. I am also putting this out there to assert that I do not believe that Nancy simply needs to "think" her way thin. Knowing what the basis of our cultural epidemic with food is all about is the first step to finding a solution that will last.

Go a layer under that and we reach the part where Nancy had been told her whole life that she was "less than" because she was obese. She confessed to me that when walking down the street she sometimes felt that people were looking at her the way Southerners looked at African-Americans in the 1950s, with palpable disdain. She felt that other people saw her as weak, lazy, and stupid. She observed it in the media all the time. And now she had painted everyone with the same brush, assuming that even if some people didn't outwardly show their disdain for her, on the inside they thought she was a lazy, fat pig. And when you hear a message that loud in your mind over and over again, you start to believe it. Nancy had taken on the role of what she thought others said about her.

Go a layer under that and we reach the child who was molested by her older cousin. The one whose mother, when she told her about the rape, said never to tell a soul, "because our kind don't talk about such things in public," and fed her a piece of blueberry pie with extra cool whip—a comforting habit that was quickly ingrained.

So what part of Nancy has the problem—her body, her mind or her spirit? I have heard many times that nature only takes what it needs, which is why you will rarely find an obese wild animal. Could it really be Nancy's being that is causing her to be obese and not her human side? I don't think so. This is where I make the distinction between the human and the animal. Even when we are not in harmony with our spirit, we are more evolved than other animals. We have psyches and complicated mind function, which do not have to be in tune with spirit to exist. In fact, the abuse that Nancy endured, and didn't properly deal with, wounded her psyche, and so do those negative thoughts she repeats to herself every day. The animals don't get the privilege of higher function but they also don't get the repercussions. Animals live in the moment. They don't dwell on the past.

What do you think happened to Nancy when I put her on a 2,500calorie diet limited in sugar and starches that only includes natural unprocessed foods? The same thing that happened when she went to Weight Watchers and Jenny Craig and Nutrisystem and L A Weight Loss and Atkins and South Beach and all the other diets. She was motivated in the beginning when she dropped a bunch of weight in the first three weeks, then got stressed over something, anything, didn't have her usual coping mechanism of comfort foods, and fell off the diet plan. Once she cheated at one meal she said to herself I might as well cheat for the whole day; well, I lost a day I might as well quit for the rest of the week, for the month . . . and before she knew it she put back on the weight she lost in the first three weeks, plus another five pounds.

Sound familiar? How absolutely frustrating is that? Almost all of us have been there to some degree. And getting off that roller coaster is as difficult as it is freeing. You know the ride: dieting and overindulging, feeling great about yourself—healthy and full of energy, and then hating yourself for being fat, lazy, and out of control. And all too often we hear the message that our weight problem is because of dieting, and if we would just eat healthy and love ourselves no matter what shape our body is in all would be okay. But Nancy is not okay at 320 pounds, her health, as well as her job and social life, are affected. She also can't just wake up one day and love herself thin. A thin body will not erase the other underlying issues of addictively reaching to food for comfort and untreated childhood emotional pain. This is a complex multilayered issue that needs to be addressed with consciousness and present-moment tools and tuning in to the higher self.

Let's introduce the *being* in human being.

Many religions address the issue of fasting as a way of being closer to God. Baha'is fast for nineteen days in the month of March, from sunup to sundown, as a means to focus on the love of God and spiritual matters; in the Catholic tradition Fridays are meatless, especially during Lent, as a means of learning to control the desires of the flesh, and as penance for sins. Buddhists, Hindus, Jews, Mormons, and Muslims all have a time of fasting or limiting what they are allowed to eat, and all these fasts have to do with forsaking the physical for the benefit of the spiritual. In addition to diet-obsessed North America, there are many cultures that do cleansing fasts, particularly in the spring, to shed the stagnant energy of rich winter food.

When I find a trend that is embraced by so many different religions and cultures, I ask myself what is the fundamental truth underneath. None of these fasts threaten the life of the body, but many of them challenge the psyche. By abstaining from food for twelve to sixteen waking hours we can get into quite a mind war.

That mind war becomes a test for our being-ness. It becomes a tool to evaluate our dependency on habits like an afternoon treat, and evaluate how much mindless eating we do in a day. It forces consciousness on us.

Nancy's obesity is not only a condition of her body; she has obvious psychological issues that trigger her emotional eating and her obesity also affects her spiritual body. *Her spiritual body is the part of her that loves and receives love.* If she cannot love herself enough to seek out the help she needs to get past this food addiction, then she won't heal. She may have thought that coming to me for an eating plan was enough—although she did suggest to me on day one that it wouldn't help as nothing else had worked—but what she eats is only a part of the battle. How she loves herself and how she talks to herself are huge parts of the equation. If she were to treat her body as the vessel for a piece of God residing on the planet with her during her journey on Earth, would she treat her body with more respect? Would you feed our Creator processed, grease-laden food or something hearty and natural that came from the Earth He created?

In addition, what she does to herself she does to the entire Universe. And when we all connect to the entire Universe, we are all cured. Will Nancy find peace when she embraces the thought that she is a part of an interconnected energy field that courses through our whole Universe? That she is an infinite soul that is only in this body for a short while? Would she treat her body with compassion and reverence if she thought of it as part of the Source?

Let me say a few words here about what we put into our bodies. Not only are we working with urges and drives in our bodies aided by neurochemicals and genes, we are also working with a Western culture that values abundance in all its glory—except for the body shape that displays abundance. I highly suggest looking up the work of Dr. Robert Lustig, a researcher from the University of California, and his series titled *The Skinny on Obesity*. His series takes a thorough look at the obesity epidemic in the developed world, the causes and the solutions.

We have moved from food in its natural state to food that lasts longer on shelves and can stand being shipped around the world. To make that food more palatable after all the processing, we add fat, sugar, and salt. We have also increased the serving size of this processed food to further our sense of abundance, and thanks to GMOs and growth hormones, even unprocessed fruits veggies and meat are "bigger and better." Psychologically speaking if we feel abundant we are prone to spend more money—marketers know this well—and that thinking has not only put a lot of money into the large corporations' pockets over the last century, it has encouraged an obesity epidemic. I will go into much more depth about our subconscious societal views around safety, abundance, and scarcity in the chapter on culture, but for now let's note that those views have permeated our food supply to the point where Nancy and the rest of us are struggling to eat healthy amounts of clean food.

I am by no means suggesting that loving herself alone will make Nancy shed 160 pounds. Nancy needs to love herself enough to put healing her self, body, mind, and spirit above all else in her life. She needs psychological counseling, dietary counseling and spiritual counseling. In fact, Nancy would do best to find someone qualified to provide both spiritual and psychological counseling together as they are closely linked.

At the other end of the spectrum, if someone were to live only in their being state, to want only to meditate, or pray, or serve others, while that sounds quite honorable and that it would be a good thing, their body would suffer, and if their body suffered from low blood sugar or malnutrition, no one would be ahead.

There is also a new epidemic of eating disorders in our younger generations, mostly children and teens who are exposed the most to our thin-idolizing media. And you read right, *children*. While we tend to think of young women being prone to anorexia, there is a growing trend for male teens and even children as young as eight years old to starve themselves for the sake of appearances.

Children are naturally more in touch with and more balanced in their being-ness. Nevertheless, they depend on adults to protect them from their environment, for example, "Don't put your hand in the fire!" and to help guide their steps: "These berries are poisonous and these are good." And as a society we have let them down. We are allowing our food supply to be altered, we are allowing society, media, and, as an extension, what we ourselves say in our daily vernacular to set an unhealthy ideal. How many times have I said "No, thank you, that will make me fat," when out in public with my children? They heard and internalized every comment.

And in this case it is not the children who need to embrace their being; it is we parents who need to do it for our children. We need to model checking in with our higher selves as we make decisions.

I will continue to reveal the effects of embracing our beings throughout this book. I know that I have only scraped the surface here. But for now let's move on to another part of the definition of a living being, the ability to reproduce.

Chapter 3

Sex

The way of the miracle-worker is to see all human behavior as one of two things: either love, or a call for love.

—*Marianne Williamson*

MY BIRDS-AND-THE-BEES TALK WITH MY DAUGHTERS went like this: "There is a gland in your brain that turns on your ovaries around grade six and makes them start pumping out an ovum every twenty-eight days. Your ovaries are biologically in charge of reproducing your DNA. Ovaries have had that job for about 200,000 years. Back when our ovaries were given that job we didn't live past the age of forty, so we had to make babies early in life. That is all that those ovaries think about—making babies. They don't care if you want to go to university first, or if you want to wait until you are married, all they care about is making you feel overwhelmingly like having sex—and this is the important part—they also produce hormones that make you smell good to males

35

who have testicles wanting them to reproduce their DNA, not every 28 days but *all the time.*"

Yeah, so they weren't all that excited about having a former registered nurse give the sex talk. But that's the way our bodies work.

Life forms have existed on Earth for about 545 million years. During this time DNA has reproduced, and the life forms have reproduced and evolved to produce the thousands of species on our planet today. Humans use sex to reproduce just as do all the other life forms on the planet. Therefore, the act of sex and reproduction is far older than what we know as consciousness. We've been having sex for longer than we've been thinking. As far as a drive is concerned, this one runs quite deep.

But we do have a conscience now and we have decided as a society that rape is frowned on, and in most societies and cultures monogamy is the rule. We are no longer quite as driven as our primitive ancestors were who used a club over the head to drag a mate back to their caves. And the species is safe at seven billion people on the planet right now.

There is also an anthropological theory about divorce and serial monogamy, that another drive adds variation to the species by causing a man to mate with different women, and vice versa. There is sociological evidence that historically a woman chose a new man after her child was walking and weaned from the breast. She would keep her husband around while she was needy and then choose another when she wasn't.

That brings us to the story of another former client of mine from my time as a cholesterol research nurse. Let's call him Lance. Lance participated in a study where I was drawing blood samples from members of entire families and taking detailed family histories, to find a genetic link for low HDL cholesterol levels. Lance was a high-priced lawyer, always dressed in crisp tailored suits, very smart and very charming. He had a beautiful wife and that millionaire combination of a son and daughter.

One day, about two months into the study, Lance walked in wearing a tee-shirt and shorts looking gaunt and grey, with dark circles under his puffy eyes. It took little for him to pour out his heart and soul to me as I measured his abdominal girth. He had broken down over the weekend and told his wife that he'd been having an affair with a legal assistant from work for the past three months. He then went into work and told the senior partners, who were appalled and asked for his resignation on the spot. In a matter of days, he lost everything. He was sleeping on his elderly mother's couch and crying incessantly. He admitted he wasn't crying because of his ruined marriage, or for disappointing his children, or for losing his job. He was crying because his mistress had broken up with him last week and broken his heart.

Most people I know would react to his story by choosing an extra large needle for his blood sample and wiggling it around a bit while poking him. I looked him in the eye and said, "Wow, you hate yourself that much, eh? You really did a number on yourself."

He stared at me, mouth open, then stammered, "I, I'm a horrible person. I hurt all of these people in my life."

I replied, "And you hurt yourself too. You chose actions that ended your marriage and decimated your career. How could you do that to yourself?"

I never expected the honesty that came from this man who barely knew me. "She was so young, vibrant, beautiful, and sexy. I was bored with my wife. We'd done all of the stuff a couple does; we fell in love, got married, had kids, had birthday parties and Christmas parties, soccer games, and ballet recitals. I was bored. I wanted to start over with the thrill of the chase and falling in love again, with having sex in every room of the house any time of day."

"All at the expense of the pain you are causing the other people around you?"

Tears formed at the corners of his red eyes. "I am a horrible person."

I said nothing at the time. I continued to take blood pressure measurements and notes and sent him on his way. Today I would tell him he was human, he made a mistake, and now he needed to fix it. It has taken me a while to get to this thinking. I have held onto that story, trying to figure out why anyone would throw his whole life away for good sex. But his is not the only case. I've known many men and women, in equal numbers, who have left a monogamous relationship to start the process over again. It has always made me wonder about the possibility of the biological drive to diversify our procreation, and our responsibility as conscious beings to think through the repercussions of our actions in response to those drives.

There are many other factors at play here besides serial monogamy. One is this lovely hormone that is secreted both when a woman breastfeeds her infant and when a man or a woman have an orgasm, oxytocin. This hormone has a nice side effect of creating a stronger bond.

Back to the sex talk with my girls; this was also a topic I covered in detail. I informed them that the principal reason they wanted to get to know a boy (or man, and I made it clear I hoped they would be grown women first) before you have sex with him is that once you do have sex with a person you form a sort of bond—similar to the imprinting with the werewolves in Twilight (they totally got that reference). I remember growing up having friends who dated real losers and they were just over the moon about how great the guys were, until two months later when the infatuation wore off, when they came to me saying, "What on Earth did I see in *that* loser?" I would answer "love is blind," not knowing that I was actually almost right. Oxytocin makes you blind to the person you just had an orgasm with. There is also a spike of dopamine with sex, and dopamine is closely linked to addiction, which I will be covering later. The moral of the story was always be choosy who you have orgasms with.

And I felt that separating intercourse and orgasm in today's day and age is important. Too often I hear of teens doing everything but having intercourse, and while that may prevent pregnancies, it does not prevent diseases or bonding with someone who can potentially break your heart.

About that broken heart.

For this, we need to lean on the expertise of anthropologist Helen Fisher who has studied romantic love on a deep biological level by using MRI and brain chemistry. According to Dr. Fisher, romantic love exists in every society that has been studied on Earth.

"It is very much like a drug high. When you're madly in love, you think this person is more special than anyone else on Earth. You focus all your attention on them. You have personality changes. You're willing to take great risks to win the person's affection. And you have the three characteristics of an addiction: tolerance—you see the person a couple of times a week at first, and that's okay for a while, and then you've got to see them every night. You also go through withdrawal and relapse with a broken heart. "

Dr. Fisher is warning us to treat a broken heart as we would recovering from a drug addiction. There are many crimes of passion around the world related to love, jealousy, and broken hearts, and unfortunately there are also too many suicides related to people—teens especially—who feel that they can't go on without the love of their lives. This is why we must always know who we are about to become attached to.

So at what point does a human say no to their brain chemistry, ovaries, or gonads? What could Lance have done differently? Should he have stayed in a marriage where he felt no passion? Can one ever have a fulfilling sex life while embracing his being-ness?

If Lance had centered himself and looked at his attraction to a new woman objectively and from his higher self, and still come up with the answer that he absolutely wanted to pursue a relationship with her, then he would have had to work things out with his wife way before he ever gave another woman his cell phone number.

While some religions and societies dictate that he should stay married to his wife until death parts them, if he were truly and deeply unhappy in his marriage his negative energy would rub off on everyone around him. He owed it to himself and to his family to be completely honest, to attempt marriage counseling to make sure the relationship is in fact irreparable, and to make retributions for honoring his need to leave this family behind. He would also have to accept and love himself for his decision and actions so as not to carry negative emotions like resentment and self-loathing into a new relationship.

These are all complicated and time-consuming conscious steps, not as easy as taking a woman out for a drink and then slipping into bed with her afterwards. But this is what being human is all about. This complexity also has with it the rewards of a lasting spiritual relationship with another human being. The depth of a relationship where both partners are aware in the present moment and conscious of the energy field around them, not only the hormonal tornado inside them, is rewarding and worth its effort.

And what happens when you don't have a choice about having sex with someone, as was the case with my ten-year-old self? What happens when your brain and body become addicted to the dopamine and vasopressin rush of an orgasm at such a young age? How confusing is it to have a bonding chemical released with someone you despise for forcing you into something you don't want?

I was blessed with a wonderful social worker when I was sixteen years old. I was headed down the road to becoming a troubled teen. Although I didn't drink much or do drugs at all, I had one-night stands—lots of them—and little respect for myself and therefore for anyone else, including my mother and sister. I was a walking, talking ball of dysfunction. The talk therapy Brian provided to me had a huge impact on who I am today. When I first met Brian I described having sex as "eating a cheeseburger," it was that casual to me, and had no deeper meaning besides satisfying a need, a drive, an urge. By the time I had done therapy with Brian, I had fallen in love for the first time with a young man named Dustin. One of Brian's parting questions for me was if my relationship with Dustin had any resemblance to eating a cheeseburger. I giggled and described what love meant to me then. It has obviously evolved over time as I have matured. I am currently in a loving, lasting, deep relationship with my husband with whom making love is special and never out of habit, and has nothing to do with cheeseburgers. Neither does being human.

The long and arduous effort of psychology appointments and self-help books and seeking alternative medicine remedies have shown me how to overcome the addiction I had to instant gratification, self-hatred, and self-loathing, to feeling guilty and thinking everyone who looked me in the eye knew my whole past, and to identifying with my past. I am being, I am now, I am love, and I am free.

Just as with food, religion has some well-defined views on sex. Some religious views are more extreme than others, but generally most frown on sex before marriage. As I said earlier, whenever many religions or cultures share a view I like to question its essence. Were the prophets of various faiths given those laws and instructions to save us from the pain and heartache of bonding with someone through orgasm who would then move on to have sex with someone else the next weekend? Was it the result of a male-dominated culture to shame and guilt women about the pleasures of sex? Was it to further divide us into groups of "good" and "bad" people, saints and sinners?

If we are to look into the deep drives and societal rules that developed around those drives, we have to examine how we categorize and ostracize people because of their sexual preferences, orientation, and identities outside of what society considers normal. Judgments lead to separation. We judge Lance for following through on a temptation that, if we re-examine our lives, we realize we have felt and may have followed through on to some degree or another. Every person in a committed relationship has felt some degree of attraction to another individual, and has had to choose to act on it or not. Some of us stopped at the fantasy in our minds, others engaged in a cat-and-mouse game of flirting and stopped there, some have gone out for coffee or dinner or drinks, and some have had decades-long affairs. If this is the human condition, why do we judge our fellow humans for walking along the same continuum? What makes some of us live at one end of that continuum and others at the other extreme?

Getting in touch with and bringing to light our deepest emotions, our highest self, and observing our choices by the light of the Source we can discern among the societal rules that are influencing our choices, the physical needs that are driving us, the games our mind is playing with us, and the highest good for ourselves and those we are connected with.

On our deepest level we want to be part of the One. We have a fear of abandonment and a fear of not being loved not only by our family or spouse but by society as well. When we are *being* we are one with the Universe and we return to our Source. We are loved. We are love.

PART 2

Sociology

Chapter 4

Culture

All the world's a stage, and all the men and women merely players: they have their exits and their entrances; and one man in his time plays many parts, his acts being seven ages.

—*William Shakespeare*

ONE OF THE GOALS OF THIS book is to empower us to find balance in our lives by embracing our biological drives with mindful choices. But how are we to maintain mindful choices over these drives if we live in a society that has control over, and can manipulate, the norms? So now, in addition to being aware of our biological food and sex drives, I am going to introduce how the environment in which we are submerged has a great deal of influence on our ability to find balance being human.

I have four beautiful children who are a joy to be raising into citizens of the world. I have always had in mind that my children were not mine. Instead I believe that I was assigned the task to guide them into the adults they will eventually become, out there serving humanity. I do my utmost to provide them with a safe, healthy, educational, and virtues-promoting environment, and I walk my talk by demonstrating the type of adult they can become. I have grown into this role as they have grown, and perfected it with all the mistakes every parent makes along the way. So it is natural to know that the mother who raised my eldest daughter fifteen years ago is not the same mother raising my youngest child today. The way I raise my children in the bubble of our home is but one factor in their lives. And as they grow older, and with today's inevitable media influence that make the walls to that bubble thinner and less opaque every day, our children are at the mercy of the culture around us.

What is the culture influencing my children and most likely yours as well?

One day as I was driving my fourteen-year-old to her piano lesson, she tuned the radio to her favorite station and as always sang along with every song. I clearly remember doing the same thing when I was young, switching my mother's sixties music to the pop of the eighties, and she warned me that one day my daughter would do the same to me. I smiled inwardly at the self-fulfilling prophecy. Then, as if I were a stranger visiting from the Jurassic period, my daughter felt the need to explain what all the songs really meant: everything from getting drunk on cough syrup to teaching the girlfriend to give proper oral sex. It made me long for the days of the Chordettes.

Later that evening, I walked in on my husband watching television. Regular, broadcast television. You know the kind that feels the need to precede almost everything besides *Dora* and

Sesame Street with a "Mature Audience Only" warning. I sat down next to him and asked what we were watching as I recognized Kurt Russell. "Soldier," he replied. "It was panned by the critics." He added, and we then became transfixed, as if watching a car wreck in real life.

The violence on the television screen was something out of a horror flick—ripping eyes out, breaking bones, blood flying everywhere. I sat there amazed that, despite a mature audience warning, so much hand-to-hand maiming and death could be allowed on broadcast television. And then, they bleeped out a curse word.

Seriously?!

You mean to tell me that my fourteen-year-old gets to learn about sex and alcohol abuse on the radio and my husband gets to have images of death and violence seared into his memory, but they are going to bleep out what society considers a not-so-nice way of saying feces? This is the culture we are raising our children in, and this is where that bubble gets so thin.

We live with the illusion that there is a ratings system protecting our children from media that is unsuitable for their malleable minds, and as responsible parents we take measures to insure that our culture doesn't negatively affect them, but at times it is inescapable.

After viewing the documentary *Miss Representation* and hearing that teens consume up to ten hours a day of media I went on a crusade to control how much my children were exposed to and tried to alter their television viewing to only include channels that had no commercials. I didn't allow fashion magazines around our home because, while there was already a moratorium against viewing violence, I also became much more aware of how much my children were being told women had to be beautiful in order to succeed.

I thought I was covered: no violence, no celebration of unattainable extremes of beauty, and limited consumerism. But let's remember that the awareness I have with my younger children now was not what I had when my older kids had full access to all the media they wanted. There are myriad factors that played into my oldest daughter's problems at age sixteen, but after researching the statistics on the influence our culture has on the choices our teens make, I couldn't help but feel that my daughter's choices were not all conscious.

- In our home city, the average age that students start to smoke cigarettes or drink alcohol is thirteen. The average age for students starting to use cannabis is fourteen.
- One in four students reported binge drinking (drinking five or more drinks on one occasion) in the past month. Binge drinking in the past month peaks at 46 percent among grade 12 students.
- Almost one in four students reported cannabis use in the past year. Cannabis use increases with every grade, from 4 percent in grades 7 to 8 to 41 percent in grade 12.
- Twenty-one percent of our city's students were offered, sold, or given an illegal drug while at school.

- In 2005, 37 percent of teens in our province ages 15 to 19 reported that they had had sexual intercourse at least once.
- Looking at U.S. chart-topping songs of 2007, it was found that one-third of these songs referenced either drugs or alcohol. More specifically researchers found that 37 percent of all country songs sing about drugs or alcohol, and 63 percent of the most popular rap songs contained references to illicit drugs.

So how much sex are teens actually being exposed to in the media?

- In 2003, 83 percent of the episodes of the top twenty shows among teen viewers contained some sexual content, including 20 percent with sexual intercourse.
- The average music video contains ninety-three sexual situations per hour. This includes eleven scenes actually depicting intercourse or oral sex.

Is it really a big deal? Does watching sex affect teens' behaviors and attitudes? According to recent studies, yes!

- Television is a source of information about sex for more than half of teens.
- The more sexual content watched on television the more likely the teenager is to have sex.
- Boys who watch violent sex scenes on television have less sympathy to victims of sexual violence.

- Girls who watch fourteen or more hours of rap music videos are more likely to engage in unsafe sex with multiple partners and get a sexually transmitted disease.

(Sources: City of Ottawa Public Health, StatsCan and parentingfamilies.com)

Why are these statistics relevant? Because our culture, through peer influence and the media, normalizes the behaviors of using alcohol and drugs, and engaging in sexual activities, and it is creating a standard of conduct, thus influencing the choices our teens make daily. Remember, the one thing teens want most is to fit in and feel a sense of belonging.

Our beliefs are what shape our reality and our choices. If we believe that teens will be teens and allow our culture to perpetuate this belief, these are the very results we will continue to see. The more we normalize it and the more we focus on these behaviors, the law of attraction will prevail every time. I heard a young mother commenting on her baby taking her first steps recently, she said her daughter toddling and tipping over was a preview of what she'd look like drunk in college. I know deep down inside that is not what this mother wants for her daughter's college education years, but our culture has put that expectation in her mind, and now she has put that out into the Universe as an option for her daughter.

But this is not only a battle to regain our subconscious programming and to protect that programming for our children, this is a battle against the people who are making billions of dollars by shaping our culture.

In the consumerism of North America, and increasingly throughout the world, we are told that resources are scarce to increase their value to consumers. The obesity epidemic didn't happen overnight, and it didn't happen because of a lack of provisions in North America. Any of the estimated forty-five million people on a diet at any given time in America can attest to the market saturation of high-fat, high-sugar convenience foods available anytime anywhere and frequently at a cheaper price than the healthy alternatives. We know what is good for us and what is not good for us. We know it is unhealthy to eat deep-fried dough instead of an apple on our afternoon break, but what is more readily available in our environment? What is being advertised? What do we associate with comfort and love, from our impressionable youth?

The commercials we see on television are not in the least random. The advertising industry is not about only designing glossy photography and creating funny commercials, it is about graduate degrees in human behavior and psychology. All ads are scientifically and psychologically studied manipulations aimed at getting us to purchase the product or service being touted. The corporate media do an excellent job of creating ad campaigns all around what we are lacking and how their products will fill the void and make us almost perfect. Their message is clear: It is all about you. And if you had whiter teeth, shinier hair, a clear complexion free of wrinkles, and a fast car, you would be loved. Intellectually you know that this is absurd. You know that your self-worth has nothing to do with the brand of toothpaste you squeeze onto your toothbrush every morning. Or does it? Have you ever felt less than while watching television? Have you ever felt less happy than all those happy people romping around? Have you ever watched television in January and thought: "Maybe I should go on a diet or join a gym"? Those are thoughts when you are actually paying attention to what is being sold, but your subconscious, the part of your mind that is paying attention when you are totally zoned out after a hard day's work, the part that is on as you are drifting to sleep with the television glowing in your bedroom—your subconscious—is soaking all of it up.

In fact, Dr. Eldon Taylor speaks of television's ability to entrance us because its flicker rate is thirty cycles per second, which induces alpha waves—the brain wave state you are in during hypnosis—and you will go into this state in under three minutes. And as I discussed previously, our subconscious mind is much more active and much more powerful than our conscious mind. Our subconscious mind is not only where our thoughtless reactions originate, it is also where habits are formed and stored, and that is exactly what advertisers depend on for repeat customers.

We then have to take into consideration the number of hours a day we as adults are exposed to media: not only the number of two-minute commercials we see in the three hours of television we watch at night, but also the product placement in those shows and movies; as well, the cultural norms they are establishing in the news stories that are frequently accused of being sensationalized or leaning toward a particular political party. How many of us take public transportation to work where we see billboards on the roads and ads on the side of buses and in bus shelters? We may leaf through a newspaper or magazine and see ads there as well. Or we have our ear phones on and listen to music. Those of us who drive to work usually do so with the radio on. Not only are we exposed to the ads on the radio stations, we are exposed to the lyrics in songs. Does your life measure up to the glorified sex, partying, drug, and alcohol use in current pop songs? Mine certainly doesn't. So we get to work, and we've already been told during our whole commute that we don't measure up to the "norm" and it's not even nine o'clock in the morning. And what are these ads telling you? That it's all about you. That if only *you* were to make these changes you would be happy. They set a false normal, one that is not attainable no matter how much money and time you invest in their products or services. In addition, quite often they are contradictory: Join the gym, and then stop in at our burger joint; we're open late.

But this isn't only since the advent of media. Historically, norms were what the clerics in the faith of a particular community preached. They had free access to ripe minds every Sabbath, and in some religions they also received feedback about how well their sermons were followed through weekly confession. Most of us have been soaking up this copious information from a young age. And we have all shaped our definition of *normal* around it, not only our normal but what is normal about others.

The corporate media and advertising companies also use psychological distancing to allow us the ease of conscience to judge others to the norms they have established. They do this by showing us movie stars behaving badly, which allows those of us who would never dare to bully a neighbor for putting their child in a beauty pageant the sense of freedom to judge others. We feel distanced enough from Hollywood to cluck and sometimes rage about how stupid they are, and we feel quite virtuous about our position. We also get television shows, like *Hoarders* and *Intervention*, which dramatize extreme mental illnesses, or extremes of misbehaved children, as in *Nanny 911*. These so-called reality shows all have some degree of scripting involved, and not only do they show a drastic example of what our society deems not normal, they give us a sense of righteousness for not being *that crazy*. Reality television has an uncanny ability to make caricatures of certain stereotypes for all of us to love to hate and talk about around the water cooler at work the next day. And so we laugh at those who are outside of the norm, and that is where the epidemic of gossip and bullying is conceived. Is there anything more divisive and separating?

Gossip is conceived in the hotbed of what is "normal" and what "should be" as dictated by society, and then it is nurtured by our scarcity world view which also increases gossip's competitive undertones. And one of the absolutely hideous actions we perpetuate through gossip and backbiting is the epidemic of bullying, especially among our youth. Because we have inadvertently made it acceptable to call others out on being outside the norm we have given our children permission to do the same to their peers through the examples we provide as adults. And the youth of today will pick on anything that is outside of the *norm*—race, religion, gender, sexual orientation, disabilities, the clothes you wear, the size of your body (too thin means you're anorexic too heavy means you're a lazy slob); you get picked on if you are easy, or if you're not you're called frigid.

Most adults would never go to a public place and make a public comment about someone's differences, but I have seen many enlightened and spiritual people make comments on social networks lecturing someone on his or her departure from what the commenter feels is "right" or normal. And in a venue like the social networks sides are quickly taken and opinions are supported, all in an effort to fit in to the norm and not be judged as an outcast.

We also have to look at how we are judging ourselves and how often we are calling other people out on things we hate about ourselves, our shadow selves. Am I saying that so-and-so is lazy because I feel lazy? Is laziness something that is frowned on in my culture? Was taking time for self-care frowned on for the women in my family?

We deeply fear being unloved; because we are all interconnected on a spiritual and quantum energetic level we long to be part of the whole—of the God Creator that breathed life into us. If we are separated from that whole we are lost and in pain. Sometimes we force ourselves out of that whole through negative thoughts about ourselves, and worse, if we stay unconscious of our actions we force others out through our judgments and bullying. We need to wake up and be aware of all the actions we take and every word we utter has to be in accordance with compassion and unity. We must be aware of the external influences on our minds and habits if we are to live peaceful, content, and happy lives. And in order to be aware of our influences we also have to take ourselves into account on a regular basis and review what we did and what we said, and review our choices and decisions and subconscious reactions. We have to be honest with ourselves, and we have to be compassionate and patient with ourselves. Deep-seated programming is not overturned in a blink of an eye, and we are always hardest on ourselves, so we can't expect old habits to change immediately.

Consider this analogy. Every single time we turn the light on in a room we get a sense of where the furniture is located. If the light goes off after a few minutes we can remember where some of the furniture was. If the light stays on a little longer the next time, we can see the color of the drapes, and we notice the cushions on the chairs. The light may go off again but because we've learned the beauty of the lighted room we work harder to get the light back on. Eventually it stays on long enough for us to see all the tiny details: the titles on the spines of the books, the vibrant colors of the fresh cut flowers, and the warm glow of the fire in the hearth.

The more we get in touch with our higher self and its connection to the Source of all, the more we want to stay there.

The solution to unveiling enculturation requires us to come into contact with our highest self and to question everything.

Chapter 5

Community

*"No life is a waste," the Blue Man said. "The only time
we waste is the time we spend thinking we're alone."*

—Mitch Albom

HUMAN BEINGS ARE MEANT TO BE social. We have lived in tribes
from the dawn of time, and for good reasons. It's difficult for one
person to be self-sufficient enough to thrive on their own. It may
be possible to survive on the land and all its bounty for a certain
amount of time, but to have a full, healthy life both psychologically
and physically as humans we need interdependence—connection.
We have evolved from tribes to separate religions and separate
nations, which feeds our need for interdependence but also
frequently highlights our differences. I am suggesting it is time to
see human beings as a tribe, a community and a common ground
for interdependence.

When Oprah Winfrey initiated her webcast online class with
Ekhart Tolle for the book *A New Earth,* she also provided us viewers

with many online resources like workbooks and journals and a search engine to create and find local likeminded individuals who wanted to get together and study *A New Earth* in a book club format. I have already professed my love of all things Oprah, and so I had no hesitation filling out the online forms to create a local book club. There were eight of us that started meeting in March of 2006. We varied in ages, in religious backgrounds, and in career paths. Eventually our numbers ebbed and flowed to a regular group of five as we moved on to study some other great inspirational books of our times.

This was not just a book club to us; this was our special community. We were a psychological support group when one of us had a crisis, we were a place to debate deep ideas of spirituality and the meaning of life in a safe and non-judgmental environment, and we were there for each other through marriages, new babies, the death of dear loved ones, illnesses, and career changes. We may live in a suburb where we don't speak regularly to every neighbor on our street, and we may be miles away from our families of origin, but we still innately clung to the idea of "it takes a village" not only to raise a child but to function as a healthy adult. And so we became our own village. We somehow knew that we couldn't make it on our own as well as we could make it as a community. We've each gone on and formed other communities to spread this wonderful sense of interdependence, and we still meet, though less frequently, each time returning to the closest thing I can call an ideal community I have ever known.

As human beings, babies need to be held, toddlers need to model older children and adults need help from other adults. Life is a celebration of dependence. Every cell in our body must work in cooperation for the whole to survive. The skin cell on my big toe may not know what's going on in my liver cell but my body provides for both of them in cooperation. As habitants of this planet we all depend on the air we share, the water, the soil, and the sunlight. Air, according to Dr. David Suzuki, is a thin layer around the planet that holds us together, that unites and links us to the past and to the future as far as we can see. Research has shown that the Argon molecule being an inert gas, meaning it undergoes almost no chemical reactions and is resistant to bonding with other elements, flows in and out of our lungs unchanged. The millions of molecules we breathe are shared by all breathing beings throughout history. The unfortunate devastation from the Japanese earthquake and subsequent tsunami in 2011 has led to debris washing up on the western shores of North-America, showing just how much we all share the same water.

So where does our current drive to break free of the tribe mentality and form our own being come from? We cannot deny that toddlers love the words "no" and "I can do it," and if you've been a teen, or raised one, I probably don't need to highlight their strive for independence. These are normal psychological stages where we learn to separate our concept of self from that of our family. As toddlers we can see with our eyes and realize that we are separate bodies, and as teens we notice that we have different gifts and talents, interests and points of view.

At this point in time, our tribal mentality is at an all-time low, in North America specifically. While, the independence from a cultural norm can be warranted in many instances it is not sustained for long. For example, if you belong to a family that believes that taking care of the planet and environment are a waste of their time, and you have gathered much evidence to believe that it is every individual's responsibility to heal an ailing environment, you are going to have to exert some sort of independence from your family/ tribe and follow your chosen way of life. But in return, you can certainly find many others that feel a strong need to protect the environment and consequently make them your new tribe, and thus entering into a new interdependence, a new culture.

Another instance of taking an independent stand would be in the instance of standing-up for someone who is in a vulnerable state. An example of that would be if the tribe of the classroom is engaged in bullying an individual, it is often encouraged to be independent of that bullying group and stand-up for the oppressed, thus forming a smaller interdependent relationship or tribe.

Independence has its benefits. It rings true to everything I highlighted as a struggle in the enculturation of humans in the previous chapter. It allows for the investigation of the truth, of our own truth and higher self. It allows for non-conformity to the group when they are swayed by the propaganda of a person in power. It allows for diversity of cultures. It allows us to be distinct. But always keep in mind that the higher self is connected to the Source and as a result to all other higher selves in the Universe.

There is a definite downside to our non-tribal culture in North-America. When you value your independence to an unhealthy level you begin to feel that you are self-made, that it's you against the world, that life is a competition, that no one has your self-interest at heart, and the worst of it, that you are hopeless if you have to ask for help.

Independence is very much an ego word, a persona, a self-image and a self-concept. When we are independent we are separate from others, as I've covered we tend to judge others in addition we think that they spend all their free time judging us. The ironic flipside is that others are overall too self-absorbed in their ego, and are too busy worrying about what you think of them to be thinking of you.

Look at our cultural surroundings, how can we not be independent? We are separate nations, in separate countries, and in our own countries we have separate political parties, separate ideals, separate social classes. We go to school and are separated from our siblings by age. The kids in our grades look different because of their different heritages and different financial means, and as I said before in almost every grouping there is a child or adult who feels the need to accentuate someone else's differentness and make fun of it.

This fear, of what others think of us and the tight-rope walk we do every day to stick to the *norms* dictated by our *perception* of what is *right* and what is *wrong*, is a negative effect of independence especially when we are presented with all these distinct norms.

The separateness also accentuates a scarcity and need for competition. The need to be significant at someone else's expense is taught from an early age with MVP's in sports and honor rolls in school, then later with scholarships, commissions checks, and performance bonuses. It's in our media as we celebrate the best of every discipline with a Pulitzer Prize all the way down to American Idol, from little league all the way up to the Olympics.

Is this independence just an innate drive? Are we born competitive, and self-absorbed? Is it genetically encoded for us to want to outshine and out-perform everyone else, or is this a wrong turn in our cultural history that has led to so many of the problems we are faced with today?

Actually, competition is not innate. Our natural state as human beings is cooperation and mutual-aid. The natural sate of our cells is cooperation, the natural state of nature and animals is cooperation and democracy and much of today's science is debunking evolution's need for competition in the survival of the fittest theory. We did take a wrong turn in culture when we misinterpreted Darwin's book as pure science instead of a theory, and we've been paying for that mistake for a very long time.

The dichotomy of being-ness and human-ness needs to be observed and unified with regards to competition. Biologically our body works in cooperation, and anthropologically as humans we have lived in tribes to cooperate and survive. There is evidence of chiefs in tribes but more along the lines of democracy than emperorship. Some believe that we need leadership in order to survive, and that without leaders we'd have anarchy and no direction. We can have leaders and not be a competition based world. If we have a committee of leaders who do not adhere to a particular ideology or separating political parties, leaders who are chosen merely for their abilities and their virtues, leaders who are not elevated above others as holding a higher more glamorous station, that committee of leaders could serve our society from their higher selves and look at those they lead in a more unified and compassionate way. This is the society of the future, this is what community will look like once we eliminate the extremes of poverty and wealth, and the discrimination of our fellow man and woman. It may not be what we have to look forward to in the next election, but once the whole of humanity realizes our innate drive for interdependence and unity we will be well on our way.

We have been taught this with the golden rule which is present in almost every religion and spiritual practice. We have always been asked not to compete with others.

"One word which sums up the basis of all good conduct is loving-kindness. Do not do to others what you do not want done to yourself." Confucius

"Regard your neighbor's gain as your own gain and your neighbor's loss as your own loss." Lao Tzu, Toaism

"Treat not others in ways that you yourself would find hurtful." The Buddha

"This is the sum of duty: do not do to others what would cause pain if done to you." Mahabharata, Hinduism

"I am a stranger to no one; and no one is a stranger to me. Indeed, I am a friend to all." Guru Granth Sahib, Sikhism

"Do not do unto others whatever is injurious to yourself." Shayast-na-Shayast, Zoroastrianism

"What is hateful to you, do not to your fellow man. That is the entire Law; the rest is commentary." Hillel, Talmud, Judaism

"In everything, do to others as you would have them do to you; for this is the law and the prophets." Jesus, Matthew 7:12

"No one of you is a believer until he desires for his brother that which he desires for himself." The Prophet Muhammad

"Blessed is he who preferreth his brother before himself." Baha'u'llah, Baha'i Faith

Chapter 6

Ego

The true value of a human being can be found in the degree to which he has attained liberation from the self.

—*Albert Einstein*

IN MY EXPERIENCE AS A HEALER, and even more as a person, I have found that our most ingrained habit is that of wanting to be right. It's all about ego. Ego is all about reactive subconscious thinking, and though it is an integral part of our self it is not associated with our higher self. Either our ego goes around fighting with everybody to be right to validate our selves, or we seek approval and do everything we can to make everybody happy. Either way, our ego is working very hard to make itself front and center—to separate itself from the whole.

Once I got re-married I left the nursing profession to start my homeopathy practice which I lovingly called Natures Insight. It seemed that as soon as I got my brochures and business cards printed I got pregnant. I practiced during my pregnancy, but found that my "pregnancy brain" had a hard time concentrating on my cases and even more difficult time keeping up with all the research papers pilling up on my desk so I put my practice on hold. After the home birth of my angelic third daughter, with a non-existent practice and a baby who slept all day while my other daughters were in school. I picked up an old manuscript I stared writing four years prior.

After a short while I decided to join a writers group. A woman I met through a workshop suggested I join the Ottawa Romance Writers Association (ORWA) as the book I was writing was about a young woman trying to decide between two men, one representing money stability and modern medicine and the other was a homeopath. I naively figured that by the end of the book I would have every romance reader alive convinced to use complimentary medicine.

At the first ORWA meeting I sat at a u-shaped grouping of tables and listened to about twenty-five women say their accolades for the month. Accolades for them were to celebrate whatever achievement they had reached that month. For some it was a new book release and for others is was the courage to send a query letter to an agent, and for others it was that they had received a rejection letter. Everyone took a chocolate from a bowl and passed it on the next person to talk. When the bowl arrived to me I had no idea what to say. They asked what I wrote and I described it as a story with a message, with a deeper meaning. A beautiful young woman named Christine, who I later learned was also a lawyer and one of the smartest people I have ever met, said: "Oh, you write Inspirational Romance. Welcome."

Inspirational Romance. How absolutely beautiful that concept was to me, to inspire others with a love story. Alas, that moment of bliss was short lived. Once I described my book to the writers over the social break, they clarified what Inspiration Romance really was, I was talking *Eat Pray Love* and they were talking a very Christian or Amish *Little House on the Prairie*.

ORWA was a huge learning experience for me. Any writing skills that I use today were honed in the six years I belonged to the ORWA family, and I owe those ladies a huge debt of gratitude. But not everything I learned at ORWA was about writing. While I was delving into *The Secret* and *A New Earth*, I was also volunteering a great amount of my free time in the running of ORWA, I did it all from snack lady to Secretary, from Newsletter Editor to Workshop Coordinator and I volunteered on many committees as well. I was dealing with up to fifty egos—plus my own.

My ego was strong. I longed for approval and worked hard to that end so when a couple of other strong egos came along and wanted to be "right", and treated most of us volunteers as employees showing absolutely no approval or gratitude, my ego was fighting mad. I ended up walking out on the group. When I left, it took three people to replace the positions I had held—that was a lot of ego I had spread around that organization. And in the end, my ego was strong enough to cause me to abandon my lifelong dream of being a writer.

My life is obviously very different today. I have put into practice what I read in *A New Earth*, I have sought out many more similar teachings and I work diligently on a daily basis to *be* in the present moment with my humanness.

That being said, our ego does serve a purpose. It is not an evil entity that we have to rid out of our lives. It is part of being human. My ego taught me about where to put up my boundaries. It taught me that while I was going around saying that I was volunteering for the greater good of the organization, I was really selfishly seeking approval. Every time that I respond to a situation from my ego I learn a lesson sooner or later, my ego is my greatest teacher.

The day my nephew was born was one of the first times I remember consciously leaving my ego at the door. Growing up in our dysfunctional family has ingrained some nasty habits of one-upping each other with insults and crude remarks. I live a two hour drive away from my mother and sister, and I could usually feel an energy come over me as I drove closer to their town. It's like a film of aggressiveness would envelope me, my speech pattern changed, the words I used changed, and I suddenly had an intention of hurting others instead of loving them. I am able to control this feeling for the most part now, especially if I am dealing with my mother or sister on an individual level, however, once the three of us were together back then all control was lost and I was the messed up fifteen-year-old version of myself all over again. And my mother was also scheduled to be at the birth.

On the two hour drive to the hospital I had chosen to ground myself, to meditate (with my eyes open) and to set my intentions for the birth of my first nephew. I walked into my sister's room in the hospital and the first thing I said was: "I have left my ego at the door. I am here for you." I got a funny look from both my mother and my sister but no nasty come-backs—a miracle in itself. Diane was in labor for a beautiful twenty-four hours. I calmly held her hand. I made her laugh when it didn't hurt to laugh, breathed with her and cried with her when it did hurt. And when it came time to push, that time where we all say the same thing: "I can't do it anymore!" I told her she could. Even though her fiancée was there and our mother was there I was the one she chose to have stand by her side, and I told her that everything that she had done in her life and learned up to now was to deliver this baby into the world, that this was her life's purpose. And she pushed out a gorgeous healthy baby boy that filled the whole room with pure love.

There are no words to describe how grateful I am that I was not reacting from habit that day. That I did not do the old routine of playing my mother and sister off each other, of blaming and belittling and berating. I did not go against my sisters wishes and insist that our mother hold her hand through the epidural, as she obviously had wanted to be the one there instead of me. I let a deeper sense of love guide me that day, and my sister often refers to my calmness, and how it was what got her through it all. Since that day, I have learned the benefits of checking my ego at the door, and I try to it much more often.

And so we get back to the harmless habits. It is clear that a habit of speaking in a hurtful manner with family was not a good habit. It was done mindlessly. If you sat myself or anyone else in our family down and asked, do you love so and so? Do you mean to hurt them? No one would answer that they purposefully want to see someone they love be hurt. But we did it so often, subconsciously pecking and biting at each other through mean words. Competition was enculturation in my family.

It took me many years to see that I carried that dynamic over to my girlfriend relationships as well. I had developed a habit of backbiting and pitting my friends against each other, with me and my ego coming out on top as the only good one out the bunch of us. Gossip and backbiting as I mentioned earlier in my examination of our culture is quite rampant, and though it has to do with the norms set forth by our society it also serves the ego quite nicely. Instead of having a unified cohesive group of friends, by talking about each of them behind their backs I was teaching them not only to dislike and compete with each other I was also teaching them how untrustworthy I was.

The whole phenomenon of Best Friends Forever (BFFs) is separating and creates competition, especially when social media is the stage where we play out our ego parades. Tweeting or writing a Facebook status about how we went to the movies with so and so, and how great of a time we had with our bestie is often aimed at showing others that they don't measure up to our fabulous ego. As always, we have to take the time and evaluate our intentions. Are we subconsciously trying to single someone out, or show someone else what they are missing? We have to choose to send out messages of inclusiveness and unity, not advertisements for separateness.

Chapter 7

Identity

It's so hard to forget pain, but it's even harder to remember sweetness. We have no scar to show for happiness. We learn so little from peace.

—Chuck Palahniuk

ANOTHER COMMON HABIT IN TODAY'S SOCIETY is identifying with, and defining ourselves by, our problems, and wanting to know about others' problems. It is disconnecting for us to take on any identity of any kind. It sets boundaries among people. How can we stay connected with others if we separate ourselves by an identity? It can be as innocuous as "I am a soccer mom," which you may or may not feel is alienating to others. It may even give you a sense of community and interdependence, which I made a strong case for earlier. But if that is all you talk about, all that you are, if that is where all your energy goes, it does keep others from connecting with you. If I am a childless executive of a Fortune 500 company, how well can I connect with a soccer mom imbedded in her identity? This example is the extreme of harmless. Other identities are much more separating and dangerous to individuals, and to humanity at large, for example, identifying with a political party and then voting without a conscious decision about the issue being raised, just to stay true to your identity; more so, taking on a national identity and blindly going to war without personally having any strife with an individual from the opposing camp.

When we identify with all of humanity, we strive to help all of humanity, we live with love and compassion in our hearts for the others in our tribe. I firmly believe this is the lesson we are on Earth to learn—how to be united as one.

I can speak with conviction on the identity of illness. Some believe they are special because they are sick and everyone else is well, so they need to be pampered and cared for. No one chooses to be sick, no one chooses to be in pain, but I have often seen people decline the offer of a solution that could remove the illness identity, especially if a person has worn that identity for years or a lifetime. I have also seen individuals refuse to search for another course of action—even refusing complimentary medicine—because they believe so strongly in Western medicine; I have seen some who refuse conventional medical care as they insist on living with the alternative medicine paradigm identity.

Some also identify with past victimization and cling to them as a badge of honor, for example, "I have been raped and you need to know that about me and to pity me." Some people don't feel their self-worth and cling to an identity that will give them attention of any kind. I'll cite a prime example of this, one of my homeopathy clients.

Susan's presenting symptoms were an inability to absorb the nutrients in her food. She was very sickly and sad, and seemed to carry the weight of the world on her thin shoulders. The routine with my homeopathy practice was to have a long initial appointment where I got to know what was particular about the presentation of illness in the client—what was unique and distinct so we could find a constitutional remedy and not just a way to relieve symptoms. I try to get a run of consciousness from my clients so they start telling me their deeper thoughts and not just what they think I want to hear. It is a skill that takes a while to develop. But Susan was not challenging in the least.

She went on at length about her abusive father and an overbearing mother, about multiple rapes she'd endured throughout her life but had never told anyone about. She recounted various violent attacks by strangers, and a suicide attempt, and subsequent labels that doctors and psychiatrists had given her which she had discounted. Every time I tried to steer her stream of consciousness ramble to physical symptoms, I heard more about her horrid past. She was a victim, through and through, and she had no way to find a silver lining. A ninety-minute appointment turned into three hours of listening to the worst atrocities that could befall one human being. I prescribed a remedy and we scheduled a follow-up appointment.

Appointment followed appointment where she hadn't taken the remedy or followed my nutritional advice, but she kept coming back and recounting her past. We eventually had a long talk about her fear of letting go of the past, her fear that if she forgot the horrors then it meant they hadn't really happened, and that her perpetrators where "getting away with it." There was also the fear that this was all she knew. Her whole life was about being a victim, from being raped to not receiving her correct change at the grocery store. She had never learned to step into her power, to turn the page and be the heroine of her own story who didn't need to be saved by someone else, to find her self-worth.

I was not qualified legally to take on the challenges that Susan described to me, and I suggested that she look into cognitive behavior therapy for what seemed like post-traumatic stress symptoms, in addition to my homeopathic remedies for her dietary issues. At the time, she still wasn't ready to let go of that identity or to face those fears. We stayed in contact, but Susan is still battling her physical and mental health issues to this day.

Although I discuss here the ability of one's mind to come over matter—I have seen it with my own eyes and read scientific studies supporting it and know that many spiritual leaders and prophets have touted the virtues of healing through belief—I also want to make a case for the right thing at the right time. There is no amount of talk that can make it through to some mental health issues if the sufferers are in the throes of a crisis or so deep into their maladies that it has become an identity.

The March I was eight months pregnant with my second daughter, I fought the snowy downtown Montreal traffic all the way from our home in the suburbs to get to a routine obstetrics appointment for which I arrived fifteen minutes late. The receptionist spoke to me curtly and scorned my disrespect for everyone's time. I turned to sit in the empty waiting room (with all those people whose time I had disrespected) and broke down into an uncontrollable wailing cry. I cried when the doctor called me in and cried for most of my check-up. She managed to get enough out of me to assess my general mood over the previous month and referred me to a psychiatrist who specialized in post-partum depression. "But I'm still pregnant! How can I have post-partum depression if I'm not post-partum yet?" Hormones are a wonderful thing, and how they do play havoc on the brain chemistry. My doctor was bang-on because I was in a full clinical depression before my daughter was two months old. I cried daily. I felt hopeless. I felt helpless, and all I really wanted to do more than anything was to run away (my own version of suicide—dying from this life and starting a new one as a stranger alone in a new city across the country).

If anyone had sat me down when I was at that point and told me that if I were to just think happy thoughts my whole life would change for the better, it would have made me both anxious and frustrated as I had no way of thinking happy and no frame of reference; my brain just couldn't do it.

Fast forward to my health and wellness career, and lo and behold, I get a client who is pregnant and doesn't want to take her doctor's advice. Stephanie had been diagnosed with borderline personality disorder (BPD), and it was suggested she attend a dialectical behavior therapy (DBT) program. She didn't want to. She didn't want that identity. She didn't want to wear the mental health label. She didn't want to be in group therapy and share parts of herself with strangers and have to listen to others and all their problems. She would much rather see an alternative therapist (I was not the first she had sought out) and find another way to live with her fits of rage and feelings of emptiness and uncontrolled impulsivity. There was no way I was going to be able to treat this mental health issue with my bag of tricks, and I knew it from my experiences with Susan. And I think deep down she also knew it, and that was part of her reasoning for asking for my help. As much as she was miserable with BPD, she also lived in fear. I had learned through my own experience how difficult it was to overcome depression and though I had taken medication there is no question in my mind that it was the alternative medicine I used right after that changed the way I think.

This time, this client actually took the remedy I prescribed. I may have learned to be more convincing, but I believe it was for the health of her unborn child and wanting to raise the baby in a calm and stable home that she risked letting go of her fears. Within two weeks she was attending her group therapy. The remedy I suggested did not cure her BPD, but it may have been enough for her to weigh her options with a clear mind. It can be argued that she was taking on a BPD identity by seeking treatment for it, but the treatment itself is an identity antidote of its own. I highly recommend that anyone with a difficult childhood or mood disorder seek out information on DBT, because healthy thought patterns are beneficial to all, with or without an illness label. The yellow pages or Google are a great place to start.

Chapter 10

Addiction

As long as we continue to live as if we are what we do, what we have, and what other people think about us, we will remain filled with judgments, opinions, evaluations, and condemnations. We will remain addicted to putting people and things in their "right" place.

—Henri J.M. Nouwen

I CANNOT WRITE ABOUT BEING HUMAN—DISCUSSING our body, mind, social tendencies, and spirit—without covering addiction. We would be hard-pressed to find someone who has never known a family member or a friend who had one form of addiction or another. And I personally feel that the way Western society is set up today, addiction will only continue to escalate. Addictions come in many forms, including well-known alcoholism and drug addiction, sex addiction, gambling addiction, smoking, workaholic, and the less obvious but pervasive eating and sugar addictions.

I am well-versed in the topic, and can confidently discuss it. I was raised in an environment ripe with alcoholics who also dabbled in the occasional illegal drug. Three of my four grandparents were alcoholic and many of my aunts and uncles have addictions of various sorts. The nature versus nurture debate does not apply in my case as both the genes and the environment are covered. And, unfortunately, addiction has moved on to the younger generations in our family as well. I consider myself a recovering sugar addict, but let's be honest, it's just sugar. I can still hold down a job and be a perfectly functioning part of society. So why am I not an alcoholic or a drug addict myself?

In one word. Fear.

One of my uncles, we'll call him Garry, is well known in our family as *the* drug addict. His name is synonymous with going too far and taking too much. We used to make wagers as to what time he would pass out during a family get-together. During his lifetime he has lost it all—spouses, children, jobs, his driver's license for multiple DUIs; he has even had a few trips to prison. Thanks to the enabling nature of our addiction-riddled family, he now couch surfs at his sisters' and brothers' and stays just long enough to become a burden before he moves on to the next. This is how I describe him today with the grace of twenty-twenty hindsight. But when I was seventeen, just starting to venture out in the big bad world and contemplating smoking cigarettes like the cool cousins and sneaking the odd drink, Garry scared me back in to my goody-two-shoes persona and altered my view of Garry and drugs forever.

Parties were common in my family—pretty much every weekend. There didn't need to be a reason; my aunts and uncles and cousins would all get together over a game of cards or to listen to music and drink. There was also the occasional drug use, especially if Garry was at the party. There was also the occasional fistfight. One night, the adults were all sitting around playing a game of cards, shooting insults at one another and laughing away. My cousin, Nathalie, and I were in my room listening to music and leafing through magazines, discussing the banalities of teen life. We got thirsty and were headed for the kitchen through a cloud of cigarette smoke and the ruckus of adults cursing when Garry started yelling at his nephew, Marc. He stood suddenly and his chair crashed to the floor while he lunged at Marc, and Marc's brother Jack held Garry back. In an instant my heart was racing and my whole body shook like a leaf, I tried to head back to my bedroom inching between the kitchen table and the wall when Garry spun around and shoved the table into my stomach, pinning me against the wall. My mind flashed white from the sudden pain. Garry had lost all touch with reality and I was just an obstacle he needed to eliminate. He soon turned his aggression onto someone else and I managed to run back into my bedroom where I vowed to Nathalie: "There is no way on Earth I am ever going to do drugs if it makes you lose your mind like that!" And I never did. Not once in my life have I ever tried drugs.

My life presented me with many more examples of why not to use drugs as I moved along my journey. There have also been times of high stress when I knew that if I were to deal with that stress with a glass of wine I would not stop, and flashes of members of my family passed out or in ruins would appear on the screen of my mind holding me back from even having one drink. I would however have no qualms about eating a whole row of cookies or a king-size chocolate bar looking for a way to cope.

Addiction is habit turned into an illness. The habit serves a purpose, or else we would never reach for those automatic responses to the cues in our life in the first place. That purpose in unhealthy habits is most often to fill a void or to numb out the anxieties and stressors of everyday life. Numb is a seductive state to be in when the world in on your shoulders, and numbing takes on many more forms than those produced by addictions.

There are some mechanical habits that are healthy and encouraged, like brushing your teeth before bed, some are harmless like patting your pocket to check for your wallet before you leave the house. These are mindless actions that we repeat over and over. The human brain doesn't pay attention to these because it has been conditioned to tune out the nonvital information in order to put its attention on the important stuff. Just as we drown out the noise of the cars passing by outside our office window or the hum of the refrigerator as we watch television, our mind is able to choose what to focus on.

Then there are the other habits. The ones that keep us mindless, numb, and distracted. There is a long list of things one can do to avoid the present moment, and as far as I know this is something only humans do—I've never seen my dog play spider solitaire. We drink alcohol, we use marijuana, we zone out in front of the television, we spend hours playing Farmville, we work too much, we party too much, we gossip, and we know more about our favorite sport team's stats than about our own grandparents' lives. Seriously, how many of us live in a state of perpetual mindfulness and consciousness?

Are we always completely aware of every action we take and every decision we make? In my opinion that is not possible. It is a good goal to strive toward, but part of being human is falling back on the subconscious as a way to disconnect from the world and cope with the abundance of information. We all do it.

So how do we know if we are dealing with an addiction or a simple numbing habit and when should we change it? An addiction interferes with the normal function of your life. It takes you away from your job, your hobbies, and the people you love.

Characteristics of addiction are:

1. A level of *tolerance* where you require more for the same *effect*.
2. You cannot find your *limits*, such as you can't stop at two glasses of wine at a party, or you decide that you will only play ten minutes of Bejeweled after dinner and six hours later you didn't do the laundry you had planned on doing, the kids didn't get their baths, and your husband is tuning off all the lights in the house and going to bed while you are still aligning jewels on a computer screen.
3. It is chronic.
4. It progressively gets worse.

Addiction, once one becomes aware of it, should always be addressed. There is a multitude of help out there should anyone realize he or she is afflicted by an addiction. The yellow pages or Google are a great place to start.

What about doing things just to fill a perceived void in our lives? Should we be concerned about these? And why do we have these voids? My answer to the latter question refers us back to the duality of being human. As I have mentioned before, we live in a world that is geared toward the physical existence and not so much toward the spiritual side of humans. And I am not referring to a religiousness or piety or new-age spiritual practice. I am talking about our deep innermost feeling of connection. If we feel disconnected from the divine love of the Universe, it doesn't matter how often we quote scripture. I feel that the rampant wildfire of addiction in our society is literally the lack of connection to something bigger than our selves.

The danger of simple numbing habits that are not an addiction yet depends on where you are on your path. Some of us are less concerned about being conscious of our being-ness, are less spiritual and content with a simple, bordering on animalistic, life. I'd feel safe to wager that those on that chosen journey wouldn't be reading this book. The rest of us are striving toward embracing our being-ness. We are concerned with our spiritual lives and our health. We want peace but not at the expense of tuning out in front of a television that will be filling our head full of norms set by the corporate media. We want true, deep, loving peace that is obtained through mindfulness and awareness of the present moment.

There is a meditation CD out there for every type of path you may wish to follow—religious, spiritual, metaphysical, angels, strictly psychology and anxiety related—they all exist. I suggest you start with that. Also take a few seconds every morning before you get out of bed to set your intention for the day, and a few moments every evening to take your day into account. Was every decision made in a conscious and mindful place? This is a great new habit that aligns us with our sense of purpose and our being. I have found it is better to face things head on with love and acceptance than to run from them in fear and avoidance. So I paid the phone bill late this month; I acknowledge this error in my timing and feel the emotions around that mistake and love and accept myself and move on. That is much more soulful than avoiding the thoughts of guilt and shame through a bowl of ice cream in front of the television. It takes a lot of courage to face our thoughts and actions in complete truthfulness, and as Mary Anne Radmacher says, "Courage doesn't always roar. Sometimes courage is the quiet voice at the end of the day saying, I will try again tomorrow."

Chapter 9

Health care and Education

It is the mark of an educated mind to be able to entertain a thought without accepting it.

—*Aristotle*

LOOKING AT THE WORLD IN EXTREMES helps us to separate by categorizing people and things and putting them into slots or teams. We still feel the camaraderie of being on that team, and a sense of interdependence, but the danger lies in its being an "us against them" phenomena, as discussed in the chapter on identity. When we see ourselves and others as something with a defined beginning and ending, there is automatically a point past which we won't go to meet the other.

I have battled with my yes/no, black/white thinking for a long time. As I have spent a great part of my adult life in the health care field either as a nurse or as an alternative practitioner, choosing an identity within health care has been a struggle for me as well, but it eventually led to my balanced view.

I often turned down opportunities because I feared the "image" it would send to others. I didn't want to be identified as an alternative healer. I didn't want to dress the part—loose fitting naturally dyed organic cotton everything, and eat the part—a vegan turning my back yard into an organic crop, and give up my love of an occasional designer handbag—the ultimate symbol of selling my soul to the corporate "man." But, I also didn't want to be identified as a registered nurse who pushed the pharmacological agenda and required hard and fast science over other healing modalities that actually work. All this time, I thought I was being noncommittal and judgmental. I was really trying to avoid the separation of different identities.

Once, when I worked as an RN in cardiology, we admitted a lady from the cardiac care unit whose heart just stopped one day. She spent an unknown amount of time unconscious, and thus had brain damage. To describe it simply, she had a whole-body stroke, she was paralyzed, she didn't speak, but she could breathe on her own and was tube fed.

The weekend prior to having Mrs. Rose as a patient, I had been to my homeopathy class. We covered the rosacea family of plant remedies, and Mrs. Rose demonstrated all the rubrics for the rose remedy.

Rewind this story about six months. I don't know about you, but I get excited when I start something new. I like to share my new findings, I want to shout them from the roof tops—it may have to do with my being innately a teacher. I had been working in the cardiac care unit when I started my homeopathy course. I was excited by all these new healing modalities I was being introduced to, and so I shared them. I posted information about alternative options to cholesterol medication and their success rates on the staff bulletin board, and I was quickly taken into the nurse manager's office and given an earful. Peer-reviewed medical science was the only thing I was allowed to discuss at work. Period.

When I transferred to a different department, I was taken into the new nurse manager's office on my first day and told explicitly that I was *never* to discuss alternative medicine with a patient. Message received loud and clear. And then the Universe sent me a patient I knew I could help with homeopathy.

So let's go back to being human. Is health part of the human condition? Is our body made to heal itself? You bet! Scrape your knee and watch from the outside with the naked eye that a scab forms to both stop the blood flow and as protection from the germs of the outside world. Take a microscope and you will marvel at your body's processes of biochemistry and how they protect the body's homeostasis—the drive to maintain equilibrium. Humans have also evolved to discover health promotion, for example, cooking their meat and large-city sanitation.

Health care as a business model is different from the shaman or medicine man of the old tribes. With monetization health care has become an enculturation and has caused firm unyielding beliefs for and against scientifically proven efficacy of pharmacological solutions or anecdotal evidence of alternative or complementary practices.

Western allopathic medicine is considered "real" health care and not the alternative only because of the large financial and political backings this modality received with the inception of the American Medical Association (AMA) in 1847. As early as 1849, the AMA established "a board to analyze quack remedies and nostrums and to enlighten the public in regard to the nature and dangerous tendencies of such remedies." Those remedies were the competition to the monetized health care of the time. Eliminating competition became a priority by the Roaring Twenties, when finances and political ties from the Carnegie and Rockefeller families sponsored research and donated money only to universities and medical schools that had drug-based research. They then went on, through their International Education Board, to extend their policy to foreign universities and medical schools where research was drug based. Establishments and research which were not drug based were refused funding and soon dissolved in favor of the lucrative pharmaceutical industry.

This history begs the question, what would health care look like today if it had never been influenced by money and politics?

To be sure, there is great value in science, and health care has made miraculous discoveries. There are in fact alternative modalities that are risky and supplements that are not standardized for potency. But one has to wonder if alternative medicine had been funded by Carnegie and Rockefeller, and allowed the same opportunities to flourish, if it too could not have advanced and become refined. Maybe if health care wasn't about profit we would have a cure for cancer and the common cold.

Medicine has become a culturally accepted first choice. My goal with this book is to find where our drives are not balanced with our higher selves. Our higher self has to stop and look at every decision we make and evaluate if it is an automatic response or an informed choice.

I struggled with these examples for a long time. Could I be a registered nurse and administer medication with side effects and counteractions the likes of what we hear listed in television commercials? Could I practice alternative medicine and deny my sick child the quick relief of a medical intervention?

My baby lies on my bed, still smelling of lavender soap, fresh out of the bath. His hair, the color of a freshly minted copper penny, curls tight atop his head. His blue eyes shine with mirth as we play a game of mirroring our tongues sticking out. I kiss his velvet soft round tummy and he squeals with delight. I can feel my heart expand with absolute unconditional love. The warmth in my chest radiates throughout my body and I know this feeling of peace and joy is pure, divine bliss.

Three days later, my baby lies on my bed whimpering. His whole body is an angry red and he is so hot I can barely touch him. The thermometer reads 40.4°C. I check: that's over three-and-a-half degrees above normal. How can that be? I just gave him fever medication an hour ago. Why isn't it working? The decision is made in a fraction of a second—we are off to the hospital. The night is cool as I drive to the hospital, praying and speeding through the empty roads. I sling my baby close to my chest and run through the automatic doors of the emergency room.

My heart has imploded. It is encased in a block of ice and ceases to beat, but I can still feel my pulse roaring in my ears. The fear I have for my son's safety is physically painful. I have to remind myself to breathe. The nurse takes my son's temperature and there is a drop of one degree. I hold my baby to my chest and his heat begins to melt the ice around my heart. Everything is going to be just fine.

Three days later, as I change my son's diaper, he gives me a grin and sticks out his tongue. Complete, utter bliss.

It doesn't matter how much education or healing experience one has; when your child is sick you panic. As a health and wellness consultant, I take the time to review the latest studies and find a balance between mind-body medicine and conventional medicine, just as I offer my clients the best of both worlds. As a parent, I find myself often trusting an innate intuition as my brain shuts down. Could my son have been given a homeopathic remedy that would have prevented our drive to the emergency room? Possibly. Am I going to beat myself up for not "fixing" my son myself? No way. Healing is an art. There is no right or wrong. I decided long ago that my children's health would not succumb to an extremist view at the expense of all viable options. All healing arts, even the scientifically studied ones, have imperfections. The more we combine them the more they will complement each other.

Could I be yoga minded and still eat meat? Could I have a natural home birth and live in a newly built house that was still gassing off? Could I still be spiritual and own a Coach bag? Eventually I learned to embrace the duality of life, to stop sticking myself into a box, to stop thinking I had to choose one or the other. I can absolutely be a spiritual being who is serving the unity of our higher consciousness and love my purple patent leather purse. And so can you.

There are many layers to the expectations we put on our children. They go out into the world as a reflection of us, their parents and caregivers, and we ask them to look good and act well and achieve. All thanks to our ego.

We are also ingrained with expectations of doing what is best for our children—giving them the best opportunities, enrolling them in the best schools, putting them in foreign language classes at age three, and music, dance, soccer, chess, and fencing, and the list never ends. If our child is gifted we announce it to the world with a bumper sticker on our car. And some parents live vicariously those unrealized dreams of pageantry or competitive sports through their children.

How is all that for pressure on us to produce perfect offspring and for our offspring to be perfect to please us? And when we feel this pressure we know it is time to stop and ask ourselves where does this idea come from? Is this from the place deep inside us that we can tap into when we are still in the present moment or is it from the fast-paced society in which we are immersed?

At what point do we let our kids just *be* kids? Their sense of wonder and magic are not an accident; they are meant to flourish in a different way at every stage of life.

Where is our responsibility when it comes to education? Are we helping or hindering our children by putting them in classrooms according to their age group and not according to their learning styles? Are we teaching our children more blind enculturation or how to think critically and come to their own conclusions? Will children's parents still get to adhere the honor roll bumper sticker to their vehicles if their children do not blindly regurgitate what the teachers have taught them and question the validity of old ways of thinking?

I am by no means criticizing school teachers. They are given a curriculum that they must work with, they are given large classrooms with students of varying skill sets and learning abilities and styles, and they are expected to perform miracles daily. This is an issue for the modern human race. We are all struggling with educating our children so they will succeed in life and advance society, and we are doing it in the context of the way it's been done for many years.

And since its inception in the industrial age, our current educational system has been largely paid for through taxation and regulated by the state. Prior to that education was for the most part run by religious groups and favored the more affluent families. Today's children's minds and our futures are therefore dependent on government policy, economy, and taxes. Teachers' unions battle it out with governments for better working conditions and wages, those governments have to make decisions on how to spend their limited money, and our children's minds are held hostage in the debate. Just as with health care, this discussion begs the question of what our society would look like if education were not monetized.

Part of the plight of teachers today is the surge in children diagnosed with or suspected of attention-deficit hyperactivity disorder (ADHD) and/or being on the autistic spectrum, in addition to a surge in learning disabilities, anxiety, and other mental health diagnoses.

All these children have gems buried deep inside them that are not being mined properly as they are labeled the "problem in the classroom" and not given the attention and instruction they need in order to shine. Even children who would be labeled "normal" by the education system's standards are not growing to their full potential in a system that does not recognize originality and independent thought. We are teaching our children from an early age to be afraid of being wrong. We ask them to not plagiarize because that is cheating but we do want them to come up with our prescribed answer, not their own version. And when you look at this in a deeper sense, it is an example of division of right and wrong, as children are only allowed to do it the way they are taught.

Are these children who need new and different education models the Universe's gift to us as a sign that we are in need of adapting and changing the way we educate children for the future? Just as health care needs to be assessed on an individual's needs and situation so should education. Just as health care needs a combination of models and paradigms so does education. Both need to return to the unification and acceptance of all of humanity instead of more separation.

Chapter 10

Religion and Politics

*In religion and politics people's beliefs and convictions
are in almost every case gotten at second-hand, and
without examination, from authorities who have not
themselves examined the questions at issue but have
taken them at second-hand from other non-examiners,
whose opinions about them were not worth a brass
farthing.*

—Mark Twain

HAVE YOU EVER WONDERED WHY DISCUSSION of these two
topics is frowned on in public? There have never been any two
more divisive sociological entities since the dawn of the human
being. Let's look at religion first, because many of us are born into
a religion and expected to keep the religion of our family of origin.
As in my case, I was baptized in the Catholic religion a mere sixteen
days after birth in order to ensure that if I should die an infant my
soul would be guaranteed a spot in heaven.

My experience with the Catholic Church growing up was through attending French-Canadian Catholic school in rural Quebec. I had a nun for a teacher in grade three and when I was in grade four the whole class would walk down the road to the church on Fridays for confession. There was a cross in every classroom and, as I recall, in all my friends' homes and in mine as well. Even today as you drive through Quebec, a tall Catholic Church steeple marks every town and many lawns are adorned with shrines to Jesus or the Virgin Mary. As a child, I connote Catholic Church's Sunday service with having to dress up, and remember that the service included directed prayers, readings from the Bible, a sermon, and Eucharist—also called Communion.

Growing up, I never paid attention to the fact that the hospitals bore the names of saints, as did the homeless shelters and most of the schools around us. I also did not realize that the Girl Guides and other youth programs I had belonged to always took place in church basements, whereas when I moved to Ottawa my daughters had their meetings in public school gymnasiums. When I lived in rural Quebec, over 85 percent of the population marked themselves down as Catholic on the census. There was little evidence of separateness that I noticed, primarily because of such a large majority.

Looking back through my experience in Quebec in the early 1980s, I can definitely see how permeable the church still was in the French-Canadian rural society since its colonization in 1608, and how much influence the Church had on "government-run" institutions. After all, these institutions and buildings had been there for a long time.

My father was born in 1939 and basically raised piously Catholic in French rural Quebec, before the Quiet Revolution of the 1960s where major changes occurred in Quebec after the election of the Liberal Party. Values, ideas, and institutions from the past were all questioned and language replaced religion as "the cause" for survival for distinctiveness in Quebec. My mother, born in 1952 and raised in the English part of urban Montreal, mostly post Quiet Revolution, was therefore not as religious as my father. After their divorce, I lived primarily with my mother who rarely attended church, thus I generally only attended with friends or with school, and as a child I never felt a strong attachment to the French-Canadian Catholic Church. I can now understand why that is so. I can also testify to an almost tangible undercurrent in French-Canadian society where we feel resentment to the church for so many years of oppression, not to mention the recent shameful uncovering of sexual abuse by priests.

But oppression is not something French-Canadian Catholics have the monopoly on; another example is the Islamic state rule in Iran, as recounted to me by a non-Muslim woman whom we will call Nora, who lived through the Iranian revolution.

Until the Iranian revolution in 1979, Iran was ruled by the "Shah," Mohammad Reza Pahlavi. The Shah was seen as being too Western and associating with the United States too much. The Mullahs (who are the Muslim equivalents of Catholic priests) spoke ill of him and his ways in the mosques and effectively started the revolution through enculturation. For some, the last straw occurred when pictures were taken of the Shah calling for a toast with the president of the United States.

What I grew up hearing as the way of life in French-Canadian Catholic Quebec in the 1600s quickly became the way of life in Iran in the 1980s. If any woman in Iran was caught without a hijab (headscarf) in public after 1980, they would risk having acid thrown on them or being raped.

There are many examples throughout history and throughout the world of religion as the cause of war, greed, and horror. Many individuals have taken issue to blind faith and dogma, to discrimination against women and believers of other religions, and to the immense sense of judgment and the subsequent guilt. No human wants to be told that because he or she does not believe what someone else believes he or she is doomed to the deepest pits of hell. Talk about being separated from the oneness of humanity!

I interviewed a few self-identified nonbelievers and atheist for this book to help me understand the difference between religion and spirituality. The main conclusion I drew was that atheists believed that social order is maintained with enculturation through subconscious learning of socially desirable outcomes—pretty much the foundation religion set through its rules long ago. Those who did have a spiritual life saw it completely separate from organized religion. It was much more of a private practice of mindfulness and oneness. This led me to the conclusion that spirituality is more of a higher-self directed activity than an enculturation or blind choice.

Religion, more often than not, also has an undercurrent of politics. There is a party line that needs to be toed, and there is a leadership that is coveted, and in many religions it holds power and prestige.

Currently in politics, there is a clear erosion of trust in the leaders and institutions of governance throughout the world. Elections have been corrupted in many nations, we find overt groups with vested interests and deep pockets having influence over candidates, and distortion in public perception of candidates and political parties is influenced by media bias. There is an emerging despair that even the most capable leaders cannot deal with the multiple problems of a defective system.

Many of us, however, crave the guidance and healthy boundaries set forth by leaders both political and spiritual. We want the safety of knowing that everywhere we go a red light means stop and a green light means go for every one of us. We want our leaders to foster justice, to drive out oppression, and to unify us as humans.

We need leaders with a true social consciousness, with a true sense of responsibility, not an overinflated ego and an identity to defend. We need to elect leaders who meet requirements such as selfless devotion and not according to personality or party affiliation. We need an influx of citizens who operate from their higher selves, mindfully and deliberately in the service of the whole of humanity, not only their own state, province, nation, or treaty organization.

This is a slow process, but the time has certainly arrived for many of us to awaken to the need of our world to change its ways. I truly believe that humans are slowly waking up, one by one, to the need to return to our spirit—not necessarily extremist religion— but a higher sense of self and higher power, a connectedness to the whole. Once we can all sense our connection to everyone and everything, we will change our old ways to find ones that protect and unify the being of man.

Since I have shared many personal stories here, I should probably also share that I no longer identify with the Catholic Church I was born and raised in, though we were not actively practicing by any stretch of the imagination. I married my first husband in the Catholic Church and baptized our two children Catholic as well. Again, we were not practicing or attending church on a regular basis; we were getting away with the minimum requirements to save our souls. We divorced in 2001, which ended my affiliation to the Catholic Church altogether.

I have spent most of my adult life a seeker engaged in a study of spirituality, and as a result I embrace all religions and unify them as one faith in one God, the Creator, the All-Knowing, the Bounteous, and the Loving Source of all Being.

PART 3

Spirit

Chapter 11

The Human Spirit

Man is in reality a spiritual being and only when he lives in the spirit is he truly happy.

—*Abdu'l-Bahá*

ULTIMATELY THERE ARE TWO STATES TO be in. One where we are connected to the whole of the Universe, to the energetic field beyond space and time that connects all of humanity, the space between the atoms where creation potential resides, the Holy Spirit, the Tao, God. The other is turned toward our lower selves, our primitive nature, our innate animalistic drives.

I have been making arguments for this as it relates to various aspects of our lives. In essence being human is the dichotomy of Spirit and Man. The natural order of life went from mineral to vegetable to animal to human, and though we share many of the same properties of the others, we are quite distinct from them and need to celebrate the special gifts we possess as humans.

As I mentioned earlier, one of the things that makes us human is our perception through our senses. It is also the cause of our separation. By defining where you end and I begin, I am able to separate you from me. I can see your form in a body, I can feel the boundaries of your skin around that body, I can hear a difference between your voice and mine, and, on a subtle level (sometimes not so subtle), I can even detect a different scent between you and me. That is the essence of the challenge of being human, spiritually we are all connected yet when we are in a body we are a separate self and not connected. We must overcome that body and its drives to realize our oneness again.

We are taught through that separateness the fear of not belonging to the whole. Not being good enough, not being loved by our parents or in a romantic relationship, not living up to the Joneses. All of this polarization that is brought forth in our social mingling is the stuff we are here to work through as human beings.

We need an ego to form an identity, yet we suffer the most when we live in an egoistic state separate from the whole of humanity. We suffer when we are not in unity and trusting God's will. Life is a movement toward our wholeness, the more we move toward God the more we are complete.

Many people would much rather orient themselves toward the orderly properties of science for fear of the unknowns in the realms of mysticism. But that is what faith is. Trust and hope. Every time we get on an airplane we have faith the aeronautical engineer knew what he was doing when he planned and built that airplane. I don't know how to fly one, or the physics and mathematics involved in getting a plane off the ground and back down again safely, but I trust and I hope. That is what I am suggesting we all do when it comes to spirituality.

Believe in the higher nature of the human being. Believe that we have been gifted with intelligence and a conscious mind that all other creatures on Earth do not possess to the same degree. Why have we been granted this bounty? And how can we deny our mystic and spiritual sides when we are so obviously different from other life forms?

It is not the fate of humans to be spiritual, it is a choice—a choice that is consciously made every time we choose to act out of purpose and not from a thoughtless reaction. It is a choice we make from an independent investigation of truth, from a keen observation of the world around us, and from trust that there is a larger and more powerful presence in the Universe that holds a greater capacity than one individual human.

We are spiritual every time we think of others, every time we act out of kindness and love, every time we are working with intention and not from habit. If you look closely you can find spirituality everywhere around you, in all your daily interactions. They may not all be moments where the angels are playing harp music in your ear, but if you look closely at humanity you will start to see the difference between be-ing human and the mere pursuit of survival. It may not be constant in everyone but the spiritual side of humanity is there to see if you look for it.

If you look hard enough you can also find cases of horrible injustice and terror in the world. I can assure you the perpetrators of these do not act in the pursuit of the virtues of spirit. Selfish acts are for the benefit of the self. These individuals are lost and in pain from being so far from the unity of God that they only know their lower natures and choose to act from them. It is the onus of humanity to ensure that every individual is shown the option of spirit and giving, love, kindness, justice, and unity. Only then can we eradicate pain with love.

Part of the problem is that we have lost trust in the confirmation of God. We have closed our eyes to the signs of the Universe working in our favor and stifled our intuition because as technology has advanced we have decided we know better, that our mind is infallible, that we don't need to turn to God. We fear the identity of religion, the dogma and unexplained rituals of the church, propaganda, and enculturation, and we've walked out on the whole notion of faith.

But not everyone needs religion to get to God. Not just one religion holds the key. Fate has given us all a life on this planet— that is our boat. Free will gives us a rudder to steer that boat across the lake of life. There are many ways we can get across the water—a direct line, along the shoreline, stuck in a circle in the middle as we lean heavily on the rudder pushing it to only one side. Religion and society can influence how we choose to steer the boat, but we do the work. Sometimes God puts a little extra puff of wind in our sails when we are headed in the right direction. And if we pay attention, we see those gifts and we learn to have faith in the process. The choice is always ours.

Yes, our lives are much richer and much more peaceful when we are oriented toward God or the universal oneness of humanity, but we live in a world that tests our orientation over and over. Picture an ellipse of a planet circling the sun, at one point it is closer and at the other extreme it is farther from the sun, but it always comes back around. That is how humans work. We cannot be perfect in our closeness to God for that is not the condition of being human. However, our goal is to make that ellipse trajectory tighter and tighter to the Oneness of God. It may be colder and darker when we veer farther away from the light, but it is a necessary part of our path. That is where the lessons are learned and that is where we decide to head back to be with God. I picture that as our trajectory tightens it will eventually look like Bernoulli's *spira mirabilis*—the perfect logarithmic spiral that can be found throughout nature. I also picture God, our creator, at the center welcoming us back home.

Epilogue

The Story about Happily Ever After

When you know better you do better.
—Maya Angelou

MY LAST THOUGHT ON BEING HUMAN is that "being" is a verb, and a verb describes an action. Being is not a permanent state it is a continual movement. It is not fixed, it is fluid. Life flows and ebbs and grows and retreats and changes direction and accelerates and slows. Stagnation is death to the human being. If our breath stops, if our blood flow stops, if our heart stops, then our body loses all vitality and we are left with a decaying shell. The old adage that it's about the journey not the destination is more than true because the destination in this case is death. Therefore, being human is not a goal. It is a process.

I have shared some clips of the movie of my life. I write this humbly as someone who, though I have learned some meaningful lessons and I love sharing them, still has wounds to heal and lessons to learn. My ego still gets seduced into right-fighting, into playing those old tapes of self-doubt, into "what's in it for me?" thoughts. But, it is by returning to my highest self and sitting in my present-moment consciousness more often that I can see my ego making its presence known before I make definite decisions.

That is the state of being human. It is realizing that you have biological and subconscious drives that have been nursed by societal and familial influences, accepting that part of your humanity, and knowing you will not always act out of conscious choice but that you will sometimes react out of fear or habit. And that's okay. I am not letting anyone off the hook to go out and plunder and pillage at will. I am saying that if you work from your spirit most of the time and make more conscious choices than unconscious ones, you can be gentle and loving with yourself when you are less than angelic. But learn the lesson. Do better. Keep the blood flowing. Keep moving forward—sometimes back, but mostly forward, and enjoy the journey of the human being.

CPSIA information can be obtained at www.ICGtesting.com
Printed in the USA
LVOW052053220313

325654LV00001B/15/P